GOD

MW00617270

SPEAKING & HEARING THE WORD OF GOD
A SPEECH-LANGUAGE PATHOLOGIST'S PERSPECTIVE

Doug and Ellyn,
Keep speaking and
Keep hearing God's
Word.

Love
Rodney

Psalm 37:4

SPEAKING & HEARING THE WORD OF GOD
A SPEECH-LANGUAGE PATHOLOGIST'S PERSPECTIVE

by

RODNEY BOYD M.Ed, CCC-SLP

WordCrafts

Published by WordCrafts Press
Tullahoma, TN 37388
www.wordcrafts.net

DEDICATION

As always, I dedicate this book to my friend, my partner in crime, my lover, the mother of our child, my wife, my Pro-Verbs 31 Woman, Brenda. She has stuck with me through thick and thin and, through it all, has been a source of encouragement in all of my dreams.

To my son Phillip who inspired me to be a better dad and example of a godly man. I pray that you saw the best and ignored the worst in me.

To anyone who has endured my teaching of the Word of God as I fleshed out these principles Sunday after Sunday in the Ruminator Sunday School class for the past twenty-five years.

To all of my teachers, educators, employers, co-workers and mentors in the field of Speech-Language Pathology who watched me grow and develop as a Speech Pathologist.

As the sun sets on the writing of this book, I want to thank Mike and Paula K. Parker for their expertise in publishing books and encouraging the writer (that would be me) to write.

Thanks to Paula K. Parker for speaking to me after I

spoke in church about words being "breath-driven thoughts" and how God's Word is actually God thoughts driven by the breath of the Holy Spirit. This was the seed that she planted for me to finish the book that I started many years ago.

Thanks to Mike Parker for gently requesting that I go over my "finished product" and make any corrections in wordage and/or the Scripture references. I found this re-reading a pleasure and found great satisfaction finding errors and correcting them. Actually having to go back and look up and read each Bible verse quoted really did increase my faith.

Thanks to David Warren, my friend, brother in the Lord, photographer who has designed the covers for my books thus far. Each one is a work of art in my mind.

Last but not least, I dedicate this book to the One who made it all possible; my Father God, the Lord Jesus and the Holy Spirit (these Three are One). Without You Lord, all of this would not make any sense.

CONTENTS

INTRODUCTION

My name is Rodney Lewis Boyd and I am a "professional student." My educational journey was filled with many ups and downs and detours. In the fall of 1970, my girlfriend Brenda (my wife of now 40-plus years) led me down the Romans Road to Salvation—various verses in the book of Romans—and my life was changed.

I graduated from high school (barely) and by January of 1971, I was enrolled in a Bible School in Chattanooga, Tennessee. I never was very studious in school and Bible School was no different. Who knew that you had to take English in Bible School? I ended up dropping out before they kicked me out, being accused of running a house of ill-repute (which is another story for another time), but the bottom line was that I became a Bible School dropout.

My next adventure in education was studying in the field of Mass Communication with an emphasis in radio (I wanted to be an educated disk jockey). This time I dropped out with a 1.6 grade point average.

The next attempted foray into school was trying to be accepted in a Bible university in Oklahoma that had a saying/motto of, "Expect a Miracle." I wrote them a letter explaining my past failures in education, including my low grade point average. I told them I understood that my 1.6 grade point average was below their standards, but I was *expecting a miracle!* I never heard from them.

I went from one job to another, never satisfied with my life. My spiritual life was progressing as I studied the Word of God on my own (sans Bible school) with a wonderful relationship with my wife Brenda, good church friends and experiences, but I was still empty in the area of my work experience.

In one of the phases of my work career, I was in construction helping to building log cabins with a company named Brethren Construction with Barry Edwards (a good brother in the Lord with a good woman of God, Beth).

One day, we were working in the dead of winter where it was zero-degree weather. On the work site we had a burn barrel with a nice, warm fire where we could warm up between building the log cabins. At one point, I was hammering a pole barn nail (a seven-inch nail) and as I struck the head of the nail, it slid down and slammed onto my gloved hand and struck my finger. I dropped the hammer and grabbed my finger, then went over to the burn barrel for a break. As I thawed out, my finger began to throb. At this point, as I was holding my finger that was still in my bloody glove, I looked up into the heavens and said out loud in front of God and all those within earshot, "Yes Lord, I hear you telling me to, *Go Back To School!*"

This was witnessed by Donnell Thompson (who was married to a woman of God named Wanda) who ended up helping me memorize anatomy terminology. To this day when I see Donnell I we will look at each other and say, "Hyoid bone?"

The next day I went to the local university, got a catalog and began thumbing through it to see what I wanted to be when I grew up. I started at the A's with Agriculture, Accounting, Aerospace, on to the B's with Biology, all the way to the very last thing available, Speech Communication.

I said to myself, *"Well, I did not see anything else that appealed to me, so I guess I will try Speech."*

I enrolled in one course, Speech Anatomy, and received an A. I progressed on and graduated with a certification to teach kindergarten to 12th grade, and went on to work on my Masters in Speech Pathology. I was so pumped to actually have graduated that I took an *overload* in Graduate School and eventually burned out and dropped out yet again.

I worked for a friend, Trent Messick of Messick Homecare (another good brother married to another good woman of God, Laura), in the durable medical equipment (D.M.E.), field but still had the fire for Speech Pathology. After around three years, I returned to graduate school and finally, finally, *finally* graduated with my Masters of Education in Speech Communications. How ironic, with my history of ups and downs in education from the first grade until that moment, I now have my Masters in Education.

NOTE: Compared to knowing Christ, my education is cow dung, which is ironic in itself as I am now teaching— and have been for over twenty-five years teaching—a class called The Ruminators, where we *moo and chew* on The Word of God like a cow chews the cud, and that ain't no bull (Philippians 3:1-8).

From that point in 1993 until the present, I have been gainfully employed in my chosen profession. As a Speech-Language Pathologist, I evaluate and treat multiple problems. Most people think that if you are a *Speech Therapist*, you only help kids say their /r/ sounds. While I am certified to teach in the areas of speech from kindergarten to twelfth grade, my focus has been in medical speech pathology and primarily with adults. I work with adults that have language, cognitive, articulation, fluency, hearing, swallowing difficulties and everything in-between.

As I grew as a Speech Pathologist, I continued growing as a Christian and began to see how fearfully and wonderfully we are made (Psalm 139:14). I began to incorporate prayer into my profession. I saw a wonderful correlation between speech, and hearing and speaking the Word of God. I realized the things that hinder the physical process of speaking and hearing, and the things that hinder the spiritual process of *speaking and hearing the Word of God*, are essentially the same things.

This book is designed to see how His (God's) *Super* can affect our *Natural*, and how the *Natural* can correlate with His *Super*.

> *"Man shall not live by bread alone, but by every* **Word** *that proceeds out of the mouth of God."*
>
> Matthew 4:4 (emphasis mine)
>
> *"Let him who has ears to hear...***hear***."*
>
> Matthew 11:15 (emphasis mine)

*"But having the same spirit of faith according to what is written, I believed, therefore I **spoke**, we also believe, therefore also we **speak**."*

II Corinthians 4:13/Psalm 116:10 (emphasis mine)

My desire is for this book to be a source of encouragement to all who hunger and thirst to hear from God and to communicate with Him, and at the same time, be able to express their faith to a lost and dying world. I truly believed that we are "wired for sound," that we can hear God and He most definitely can hear us. It is in the tension of this inter-personal communication where He can be manifested in our everyday, nitty-gritty world. You don't have to put your mind on hold or commit intellectual suicide to be a follower of Jesus.

Rodney Boyd - Speech Language Pathologist
M.Ed; CCC-SLP
Masters of Education
Certificate of Clinical Competence

CHAPTER ONE
FEARFULLY AND WONDERFULLY MADE

"For Thou didst form my inward parts; Thou didst weave me in my mother's womb, I will give thanks to Thee, for I am fearfully and wonderfully made; Wonderful are Thy works and my soul knows it very well."

Psalm 139:13-14

We are either a cosmic accident or we are created beings who have been created by the grand design of the Grand Creator. The complexities of who we are as human beings are the result of either a "big bang" or by a "spoken word." The old joke is that, "Christians do believe in the big bang; God spoke, and *Bang!* Creation happened."

"In the beginning God created the heavens and the earth."

Genesis 1:1

There are various words from Genesis 1:1 to Genesis 2:25 that describe the Creator in the creation process including:

- Created
- Said
- Let/Allow there to be

- Called
- Made
- Placed
- There was
- Blessed
- Given
- Dominion/Rule
- Formed
- Breath
- Caused
- Took and Put
- Commanded
- Caused

The initial Creator-to-human-creation-connection was with an inanimate lump of clay and the breath of God. The cause-and-effect of this connection was an animated human being, a living soul. Some say—and I am one of them who believes—that this is the first incident of C.P.R. (Cardiopulmonary Resuscitation). Of course, to be resuscitated you have to be breathing in the first place, and this was the first breath to jump start the lump of clay.

> *"Then the Lord God formed man of dust from the ground, and breathed into his nostrils the breath of life; and man became a living being/soul."*

Genesis 2:7

BREATHED: nâphach (naw-fakh') - A primitive root; to puff, in various applications (literally, to inflate, blow hard, scatter, kindle, expire; figuratively, to disesteem): - blow, breath, give up, cause to lose [life], seething, snuff. (*Strong's*)

BREATH: neshâmah (nesh-aw-maw') - a puff, that is, wind, angry or vital breath, divine inspiration, intellect or (concretely) an animal: - blast, (that) breath (-eth), inspiration, soul, spirit. nâsham (naw-sham') - A primitive root; properly to blow away, that is, destroy: - destroy. (*Strong's*)

The cause-and-effect of the breath of God is a living being/soul. The Spirit of God on human flesh initiated life and relationship.

This was God's grand design which included man, wo-man, hu-man. God the Creator, created male and fe-male, man and wo-man. Not only did God create these beings, He gave both dominion and authority on planet Earth to the ones that He had created.

> "Then God said, 'Let Us make man in Our image, according to Our likeness; and let them rule over the fish of the sea and over the birds of the sky, and over the cattle and over all the earth, and over every creeping thing that creeps on the earth. And God created **man** in His own image, in the image of God He created him; **male** and **female** He created them. And God blessed them; and God said to them, 'Be fruitful and multiply, and fill the earth, and subdue it; and rule over the fish of the sea and over the birds of the sky, and over every living thing that moves on the earth.' Then God said, 'Behold, I have given you every plant yielding seed that is on the surface of the earth and every tree which has fruit yielding seed; it shall be food for you, and to every beast of the earth and to every bird of the sky and to everything that

moves on the earth which has life, I have given every green plant for food; and it was so."

Genesis 1:26-30 (emphasis mine)

We see that the Grand Design—the Blueprint for human beings—was God Himself. Words like "Us" and "Our" points, in my mind, to the Father, the Son, and the Holy Spirit.

We see in this creative process that *breath* was the intricate component of the connection between man and God. In the speech process, breath is the intricate component of the connection between thought and *speech*. Verbal expression is made possible by the inhalation/exhalation process of the respiratory system.

CHAPTER TWO
THE MAKEUP OF THE CREATED BEING

*"Now may the God of peace Himself sanctify you entirely;
and may your spirit* **(pneuma)** *and soul* **(psuche)** *and
body* **(soma)** *be preserved complete without blame at the
coming of our Lord Jesus Christ."*

I Thessalonians 5:23
(*Strong's* reference mine)

The human unit is comprised of three parts. According to
Scriptures, we are (1) spirit (2) soul (3) body.

People who worship themselves as human beings, in the
religion of Humanism tend to believe that we are *not*
created and are nothing but a byproduct of a cosmic
accident. They believe that there was a primordial ooze
that, when met with a superhot reaction with a big bang,
caused (not created) a slime that crawled out of the
waters, grew a tail, climbed a tree, hung by the tail and—
when the tail fell off—the slime stood up and *Bang!* man
stood upright. Harold Hill had a book that described this
called, *From Goo to You by Way of the Zoo.* The *theory* of
evolution attempts to explain this process by
circumventing the potential for the Creator. The sad thing

about this thing called evolution is that as mankind progresses with intelligence and productivity in our existence, we are spiritually in a downward spiral of de-evolution.

As we have seen in Chapter One, we are created by a Creator who used Himself as the blueprint for this Grand Design. We are beginning to see that this lump of clay is much more complicated than a physical body that walks around living like a creation of Victor Frankenstein (or *'Franken-steen'* for you Mel Brooks fans). We are an interconnected being of three parts that acts as one unit.

For teaching purposes, we will be breaking it down into individual units; but again, we are as human beings, one being with three parts. In the natural we will be looking more specifically at the speaking and hearing components in the natural, and relating principles about the spiritual.

spirit

soul

body

MAN - TEMPLE OF THE HOLY GHOST

Let's take a look at the Hebrew and Greek words for spirit, soul and body. We will start with the Greek words found in I Thessalonians 5:23 and then after each one we will look at the Hebrew words.

SPIRIT (Greek) (Human and Holy) Pneuma (pnyoo'-mah)=From G4154; a current of air, that is, breath (blast) or a breeze; by analogy or figuratively a spirit, that is, (human) the rational soul, (by implication) vital principle, mental disposition, etc., or (superhuman) an angel, daemon, or (divine) God, Christ's spirit, the Holy spirit: - ghost, life, spirit (-ual, -ually), mind. G4154: pneo (pneh'-o)=A primary word; to breathe hard, that is, breeze: - blow. (*Strong's*)

SPIRIT (Hebrew): ru ach (roo'-akh)=From H7306; wind; by resemblance breath, that is, a sensible (or even violent) exhalation; figuratively life, anger, unsubstantiality; by extension a region of the sky; by resemblance spirit, but only of a rational being (including its expression and functions): - air, anger, blast, breath, X cool, courage, mind, X quarter, X side, spirit ([-ual]), tempest, X vain, ([whirl-]) wind (-y). H7306: ru ach (roo'-akh=A primitive root; properly to blow, that is, breathe; only (literally) to smell or (by implication perceive (figuratively to anticipate, enjoy): - accept, smell, X touch, make of quick understanding. (*Strong's*)

NOTE: The breath of a human being—where we inhale and we exhale—was, as we said earlier, is what jump started us to being alive. We became a "living soul" as a result of the breath of God, the pneuma/ruach from God's lips to man's nostrils. The inflation of the lungs with the breath of God and breathing in and out remains a divine connection to this day. King David put it this way, *"Let everything that has breath praise the Lord. Praise the Lord!"* (Psalm 150:6) Wayne Berry, who is the Worship Pastor at my church, and whom I like to refer to as a Sonic Ninja, puts it this way, "Are ya' breathing? Selah!" Sometimes, when the pressures of life surround me, and the voices of the world scream at me, I like to take a deep breath and release it and connect with the Creator.

SOUL (Greek): psuche   (psoo-khay')=From G5594; breath, that is, (by implication) spirit, abstractly or concretely (the animal sentient principle only; thus distinguished on the one hand from G4151, which is the rational and immortal soul; and on the other from G2222, which is mere vitality, even of plants: these terms thus exactly correspond respectively to the Hebrew [H5315], [H7307] and [H2416]: - heart (+ -ily), life, mind, soul, + us, + you. G5594: psucho   (psoo'-kho)=A primary verb; to breathe (voluntarily but gently; thus differing on the one hand from G4154, which denotes properly a forcible respiration; and on the other from the base of G109, which refers properly to an inanimate breeze), that is, (by implication of reduction of temperature by evaporation) to chill (figuratively): - wax cold. (*Strong's*)

SOUL (Hebrew): Nephesh   (neh'-fesh)=From H5314; properly a breathing creature, that is, animal or (abstractly) vitality; used very widely in a literal, accommodated or figurative sense (bodily or mental): - any, appetite, beast, body, breath, creature, X dead (-ly), desire, X [dis-] contented, X fish, ghost, + greedy, he, heart (-y), (hath, X jeopardy of) life (X in jeopardy), lust, man, me, mind, mortality, one, own, person, pleasure, (her-, him-, my-, thy-) self, them (your) -selves, + slay, soul, + tablet, they, thing, (X she) will, X would have it. H5314: na   phash

13

(naw-fash')=A primitive root; to breathe; passively, to be breathed upon, that is, (figuratively) refreshed (as if by a current of air): - (be) refresh selves (-ed). (*Strong's*)

NOTE: The soul is described as, 'the seat of our emotion.' In our culture, the term 'soul' has been used to describe a Black American's experience (good, bad or ugly) and is expressed musically as blues, rhythm and blues, or soul music. It is also descriptive of a type of food, and also emotions of love as in 'heart and soul.' If someone of the Caucasian race exhibits qualities of the Black experience, some call it, "blue eyed soul." One of my favorite songs by Sam and Dave and later covered by the Blues Brothers is *Soul Man*. In 1969, back in the day when music had an increasing spiritual flavor to it, Lawrence Reynolds had a hit (that was covered by many) called, *Jesus Is a Soul Man*.

The word 'soul' (psuche) is where we get the word *psyche*…and words like *psychology*. It has come to describe our (1) mind (how we think), (2) volition (free will/choice) and (3) emotions (the gauge of how we feel). We also describe our soul in relationship to our body (soma), as how the emotions affect our physical being with the word psychosomatic.

BODY (Greek): so ma (so'-mah)=From G4982; the body (as a sound whole), used in a very wide application, literally or figuratively: - bodily, body, slave. G4982: so zo (sode'-zo)=From a primary word σω□ ς so s (contraction for the obsolete σα□ ος saos, "safe"); to save, that is, deliver or protect (literally or figuratively): - heal, preserve, save (self), do well, be (make) whole. (*Strong's*)

BODY (Hebrew) nebe la h (neb-ay-law')=From H5034; a

flabby thing, that is, a carcase or carrion (human or bestial, often collective); figuratively an idol: - (dead) body, (dead) carcase, dead of itself, which died, (beast) that (which) dieth of itself. H5034= na be 1 (naw-bale')=A primitive root; to wilt; generally to fall away, fail, faint; figuratively to be foolish or (morally) wicked; causatively to despise, disgrace: - disgrace, dishonour, lightly esteem, fade (away, -ing), fall (down, -ling, off), do foolishly, come to nought, X surely, make vile, wither. (*Strong's*)

NOTE: We are made up of flesh, blood, bones, organs, nerves, cells, all interconnected to make up the human physical component. Elvis Presley had a song in his favorite—and mine also—movie, *King Creole*. The song was *Trouble*. In the song, Elvis sings that he is only flesh, blood and bones and recommends that if you're looking for trouble to not come alone.

This is a great song; but bad theology. As we have seen we are *not* just flesh, blood and bones, but we are also spirit and soul. There are a few more things that I would like to look at in reference to our spirituality and our physical being and the connection of the three-as-one unit. There is a distinction between the human spirit and the Holy Spirit (the Spirit of God) that utilizes the same word, pneuma. Both involve breath/wind; but one cannot function with the other, and the other functions as a result of one.

Bruce Coble, my pastor, mentor, and friend, describes the relationship between the body and God as, "We are nothing but lumps of clay filled with the breath of God."

The human spirit is known as the "lamp/candle of the

Lord."

> *"The spirit of man is the lamp/candle of the Lord, searching*
> *all the innermost parts of his being."*
>
> Proverbs 20:27

NOTE: A lamp (the human spirit, 'little *s*') is a clay vessel that houses oil (symbolic of the Holy Spirit, 'big *S*'). When the wick is lit, there is light, illumination, an atmospheric change in a room, intimacy between people.

The spirit (little *s*) of man searches the innermost part of his being. The core, the center of this shell we call the human body is the human spirit, that is the connection point with the Creator of the universe. According to the Apostle Paul, there is a point of revelation of spiritual things.

> *"But just as it written, things which eye has not seen and ear*
> *has not heard and which have not entered the heart of man,*
> *all that God has prepared for those who love Him."*
>
> I Corinthians 2:9

Words like eye, ear, heard, are words that speak of the physical being/the soma/the body. But God has things prepared to be experienced via the spiritual portal, the human spirit, the lamp of the Lord.

> *"For to us God revealed them through the Spirit **(big S)**,*
> *for the Spirit **(big S)** searches all things even the depths of*
> *God. For who among men knows the thoughts of a man*
> *except the spirit **(little s)** of the man, which is in him? Even*
> *so, the thoughts of God no one knows except the Spirit **(big**
> ***S)** of God. Now we received not the spirit **(little s)** of the*
> *world, but the Spirit **(big S)** who is from God, that we*
> *might know the things freely given to us by God, which things*

*we also speak, not in words taught by human wisdom, but in those taught by the Spirit **(big S)** combining spiritual thoughts with spiritual words."*

I Corinthians 2:10-13 (emphasis mine)

We see that the Spirit (big *S*) is a teacher of spiritual words. Communication with God Himself, via the Holy Spirit (big *S*) deep in our soma (physical body) into what is known as our *innermost being* or *belly* according to Proverbs 20:27 and John 7:38.

INNERMOST BEING/BELLY: Bet en (beh'-ten)=From an unused root probably meaning to be hollow; the belly, especially the womb; also the bosom or body of anything: - belly, body, + as they be born, + within, womb. (*Strong's*)

Another incident of the physical and spiritual interacting is with the mother of Jesus, Mary. She receives word from an angel that she will give birth to the Messiah, and after the initial response of, *"how can this be,"* she tells Gabriel, *"...let it be done to me according to your word."* (Luke 1:38) Of course the word of the messenger was the Word of The Lord. Mary later sang a song known as *The Magnificat*: *"My* **soul** *exalts the Lord, and in my* **spirit (little s)** *has rejoiced in God my Savior."* (Luke 1:46-47 emphasis mine)

Another passage of Scripture shows the relationship of the Word of God and the intricacy of the human being both spiritual and physical.

"For the **Word of God** *is living and active and sharper than any two-edged sword and piercing as far at the division of* **soul** *and* **spirit**, *of both joints and* **marrow**, *and able to judge the* **thoughts** *and* **intentions of the heart."***

Hebrews 4:12 (emphasis mine)

We now will begin to look at the physical abilities of speaking and hearing in the natural and then look at speaking and hearing in the spiritual realm and what causes problems in both areas.

As a Speech-Language Pathologist, I have been trained in the development of Speech and Hearing and the things that would hinder the natural progress of development. I have also been trained in how to evaluate and then treat the problems for increasing the maximum abilities of the communication potential. This also includes dis-order, dis-ease, and dys-function of (and not limited to):

- Language
- Articulation
- Hearing
- Dysphagia (swallowing)
- Talking/Speech
- Breath Control
- Apraxia (motor control)
- Aphasia (language difficulties)
- Voice (the larynx for sound production)
- Stuttering
- Cognitive Communication

As a Speech-Language Pathologist, we study how things are developed, how they function properly and—when they don't function properly—how we can treat the problem. As with the nature of medicine and behavioral issues, we tend to focus on the problem and not the root or cause of the problem. We mask symptoms until those same symptoms flair up again and again. We are like detectives, looking for clues and piecing together solutions.

We are created to operate in (1) ease (2) order and (3) function, but—with the advent of the sin of disobedience in the Garden—our *speech* suffers with (1) dis-ease (2) dis-order (3) dys-function. (*Thanx and a Tip o' Da Hat to Dr. Peter Camilio of Revolution Chiropractic and Maximized Living for these insights*).

CHAPTER THREE
THE NATURAL SPEECH PROCESS

"And they were utterly astonished saying, 'He has done all things well; He makes even the deaf to hear, and the dumb to speak.'"

Mark 7:37

Once again, allow me to underscore that, "we are fearfully and wonderfully made."(Psalms 139:13-14) The speech process is a complicated and intricate series of events. We don't have to think through the process step by step, but we flow in the reflexive actions that were set into motion back in the Garden. It is hard to separate the *speech process* and the *hearing process*, but we will for our purposes in a later chapter.

This lump of clay (the human body) with 15+ physical parts of the anatomical speech structure is what is needed to produce speech. The speech process starts with the same process that happened at the point of creation of man; breath/pneuma. The brain is the unseen component in this diagram that would make part number 16.

In Chapter One, we spoke of being "fearfully and

wonderfully made" versus being some kind of a cosmic accident. As we look at the speech and hearing process, this wonderful intricate, articulate, synergistic, sequential, physical act, becomes even more wondrous than before.

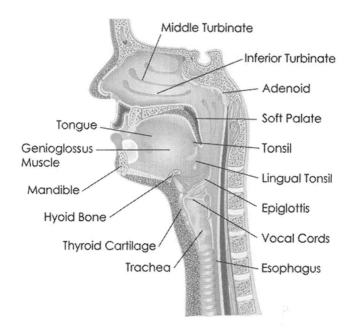

BREATH

The act of breathing is integral to what we call "living." We go through life with this rhythmic reciprocity of air exchange over and over again. We inhale oxygen and then we exhale waste gases, including carbon dioxide through this ventilation process. The simple act of breathing can be thought of as the teamsters of the body, delivering oxygen and removing carbon dioxide throughout our vital systems. It also is the catalyst for blood movement, that the Bible calls "life in the blood."

"For the life of the flesh (body) is in the blood, and I have given it to you on the altar to make atonement for your souls; for it is in the blood, by reason of the life that makes atonement."

Leviticus 17:11

We see in the transition from the Old Testament to the New Testament that this atonement for our sins is made through the blood of Jesus and not bulls and goats.

"But when Christ appeared as a high priest of the good things to come, He entered through the greater and more perfect tabernacle, not made with hands, that is to say, not of this creation; and not through the blood of goats and calves, but through His own blood, He entered the Holy Place once for all, having obtained eternal redemption. For if the blood of goats and bulls and the ashes of a heifer sprinkling those who have been defiled, sanctify for the cleansing of the flesh, how much more will the blood of Christ, Who through the eternal Spirit offered Himself without blemish to God, cleanse your conscience from dead works to serve the living God?"

Hebrews 9:11-14

In the physical body, it is the breathing process that propels oxygen throughout the body and moves the life-giving blood. In our spiritual realm, it is the breath of God that propels the life-giving blood of Jesus to infuse life into our being.

LARYNX (lair-inks)

One of the most mispronounced words for a speech mechanism is the larynx. It is pronounced lair-inks and not lair-nicks. Of course, the most famous person to mispronounce the word is Barney Fife as he describe the singing process and the need for care of his larynx.

The larynx is an interesting mechanism. It is a combination of cartilage and muscles and is the point where our vocal folds are located. It is known as the *voice generator*. With the flow of the exhalation of air from the lungs, that was just inhaled, the breaking apart of vocal folds produces sound. As oxygen is inhaled and passes through the open (abducted) vocal folds (not cords) there is what is known as the Bernoulli's principle or effect, where the draw of air passing through the vocal folds initiates the closing (adduction) of the vocal folds (in combination with the nervous system) and—as the closed vocal folds are broken apart by airflow—sound is produced. It has been said that if you cut off your head at the level of the larynx, the sound would sound like a Bronx cheer or a whoopee cushion. Of course, this is pure conjecture; once the head is cut off, there is no airflow. One of the reasons we sound the way we do as individuals is because our vocal folds are tuned to certain frequencies. Combined with our individual resonating cavities, this creates the unique sound that people consider to be *us*. Keep in mind; God knows our frequencies and resonance levels, and hears us perfectly.

When you are not talking, as the air flows in and out of the laryngeal gatekeeper, there is no sound produced. It is only when the vocal folds are set into motion, that sound or noise is produced.

A little side note (aka a bunny trail): while the larynx and vocal folds are producers of sounds, that is not their primary function. The primary function is safety, to keep anything from entering the lungs. While you swallow food or liquids, the vocal folds close tightly, the epiglottis covers the closed vocal folds, and the food or drink passes over the larynx into the esophagus. The trachea and the esophagus are known as "the wind pipe" and the "food pipe." When something goes down the "wrong way" and we begin to cough and/or choke, people often say, "that went down the wrong pipe." The wrong pipe is the trachea via the larynx, and the right pipe is the esophagus via the cricopharyngeal muscle.

Other uses for the larynx with the subglottic (below the glottis or opening of the larynx) is for giving birth to babies (push, push), using the bathroom for #2 (think *grunt*), and lifting heavy objects (be sure to use your legs and not your back when lifting). Wow, that little thing in our throat is very useful. Did I mention to you that we are fearfully and wonderfully made/created? (Psalm 139:14)

We think a thought, breathe in and breathe out and now that thought is ready to be expresses verbally. We will see later, in conjunction with spiritual words, that we have Spirit driven thoughts resulting in spiritual words. For now, our generated sound flows through resonating cavities.

RESONATING CAVITIES

Resonance is the sound after it passes through the resonating cavities of our throat and head. The sound each person makes is based on the shape of these cavities in their throat and head; everyone's resonating cavity is shaped differently.

The pharyngeal cavity, commonly known as the throat, is the first exit passage of the sound. As the sound flows upward, it comes to a split in the pathway of the sound into (1) the oral cavity (2) the nasal cavity. Depending on the phonetics of the sound, certain sounds will be blocked or received.

The gatekeeper for these sounds is the soft plate. This is the extension off of the hard palate (the roof of the mouth) and, as implied, is softer. When not speaking, it is at rest but, with certain sounds, it springs into action and elevates itself to block the sound from entering the nasal passage or stays open to allow sounds to enter. When it is closed, sound is diverted into the oral cavity (mouth).

On the tip of the soft palate is what is known as the uvula or the velar tail. We have mentioned Barney Fife on *The Andy Griffith Show* mispronouncing the word larynx, but he also had some wisdom about this thing called the uvula.

"I got a uvula, you got a uvula, all God's children got a uvula."

The uvula is that little thingy (my technical term) that hangs from the end of the soft palate.

THE NASAL PASSAGE

The nasal passage is the entrance way for oxygen to enter into our bodies (unless you are a mouth breather). It is where the resonance of the sound quality will be for sounds produced from the nose, such as /n/, /m/, and /ing/ sounds. Nasal resonance can be normal, hyper (over) nasal, or hypo (below) nasal.

In addition to resonance during the phonation (speaking) process, other uses of the nasal passage include (1) humidification of the inflowing air, (2) warming the inflowing air and (3) capturing of foreign objects by the cilia (little tiny hairs).

THE ORAL CAVITY

The oral cavity (the mouth) is where the flow of sound is

shaped and gives quality of sound to what we speak. Again, part of the oral cavity is the velum (soft palate). Within the oral cavity are what is known as articulators. These are also known as organs of the speech mechanism and produce "meaningful sound" for speech. The articulators include:

- Lips
- Lower jaw
- Velum
- Tongue
- Pharynx
- Cheeks
- Fauces
- Hyoid bone
- Larynx
- Uvula
- Alveolar ridge
- Nose
- Teeth
- Sinuses

The articulation (where things touch or connect) produces what is known as articulation. Let me clarify this for those who think that sentence sounds grammatically incorrect. In speech, when an object touches another item it is said *to articulate*. For example, bone touches bone it articulates thus the point articulation. When the tip of the tongue touches any area to make a sound, it articulates. So things like teeth, tongue, alveolar ridge, hard palate, soft palate, lips are all called articulators. When we voice once the articulators articulate; it is called articulation. The articulators take the stream of air and generated sound and opens and closes producing distinct sounds that collectively form words. This is where we enunciate.

"The rain in Spain falls mainly on the plain." Eliza Doolittle says precisely.

"I think she's got it! I think she's got it!" exclaims Professor Higgins to Colonel Pickering.

Eliza repeats the sentence again and he says "By George, she's got it! By George, she's got it!" (From *My Fair Lady* as Professor Higgins and Colonel Pickering drilled Eliza Doolittle to change her Cockney dialect.)

"How do you do Mrs. Wiley?" (Ernest T. Bass practicing his speech with Barney and Andy on the *Andy Griffith Show*).

NOTE: Mrs. Wiley detected his accent as being, "Definitely back bay Boston."

When there is a disruption of any of the musculature or processes that we have mentioned, there is a dis-ease, dis-order, dys-function of the speech process. This is where a Speech-Language Pathologist is called in to evaluate and treat the patient and help restore speech ease, order, and function.

This might be a good place to mention that a Speech-Language Pathologist is not necessarily medical in nature, even though we are involved in medical issues. Specifically, we deal with behavioral issues of speech production. Behavior or habits can be reorganized by means of neuroplasticity in conjunction with natural healing processes set into motion by the Creator. Neuroplasticity (aka brain plasticity) is changes in neural pathways and synapses due to changes in behavior, environment, neural processes, thinking and emotions.

Now, let us look at the hearing process and then we will look at spiritual speech and hearing process.

CHAPTER FOUR
THE NATURAL HEARING PROCESS

As we look at the intricate process of hearing sound, we will continue to see (and hear) that we are fearfully and wonderfully made.

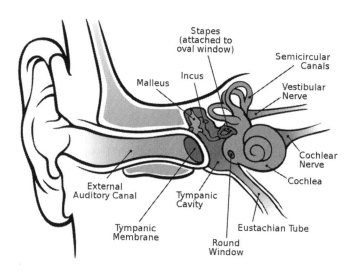

For us to hear something, we must have a sound source. This can range from the spoken word to the vocal folds vibrating. For sound to be heard, there must be a receiver of the sound, and that thing is known as the ear. On our head (aka the noggin), we have two flaps on the side of our head bilaterally (one on each side). Ears are as individual as the person on whom they are attached. Ears are big, small, medium, some very ugly, some pristine and perfect.

This thing called sound goes through several changes before we can actually hear sound and go through the process of perception of sound and understanding what we have heard. The process which we will look at includes:

- Aerodynamic (sound traveling through the air)
- Mechanical (the three bones set into motion in the middle ear when sound strikes the tympanic membrane)
- Hydraulic (the movement of fluid set into motion when the last bone of the middle ear goes in and out)
- Electric (as the hair in the inner ear shell snaps and sparks energy along the cochlea (the snail like bone) that has various frequencies along the way.
- Neural (that is sent to the brain via the VIII Cranial Nerve [the Acoustic Nerve])

What an intricate process of how sound is received by this thing called our ear. Again, did I mention that we are fearfully and wonderfully made? (Psalm139:14)

As Jesus was sharing truth with His disciples, He would often say,

> *"He who has ears to hear, let him hear."*

Matthew 11:15

Jesus was speaking of those who have the flaps on the side of your head—and the ability to hear His words—to actually hear *within* the truth He was speaking. It could be said this way;

> *"He who has pinna/auricles (flaps on the side of your head) to capture sound, let him perceive and understand what is being physically spoken."*
>
> Matthew 11:15 (my emphasis and spin on it)

The outer ear (aka the pinna or auricle) is where most people think hearing occurs. But really, the out ear is merely the collector of sound. Once the sound is collected, it is directed down to the real hearing mechanisms via the ear canal. The sound then strikes what is known as the tympanic membrane, also known as the ear drum. The sound striking the ear drum then sets into motion three of the smallest bones in the body, the (1) malleus/hammer (2) incus/anvil and (3) stapes/stirrup. The names *hammer, anvil* and *stirrup* are based on the shapes of the bones.

This jointed movement of the three bones will set into motion, within the inner ear (the cochlea), this thing we call sound.

The stapes is connected to the cochlea in a water tight connection that moves the fluid in the inner ear that follows the route of the snail like shape and causes little tiny hairs (cilia) to snap and spark. Along this snail like route, these areas are tuned to certain frequencies ranging from low to high sounds. Once the cilia are snapped, the electrical energy is sent via the VIII Cranial Nerve to the area where acoustic signals are received in the temporal lobe of the brain. At this place the sound is translated, decoded and then encoded and sent back so that we can respond to what we have heard.

Did I mention that we are fearfully and wonderfully made? (Psalm 139:14)

Also in the inner ear are the organs of balance called the Utricle and Saccule. This is where the sensation of vertigo is generated. These are part of what is known as the Vestibular system which is key for balance/equilibrium. This system includes:

- Saccule
- Utricle
- Three semicircular canals
- Fluid called endolymph and perilymph fluids

This is like an internal gyroscope to keep us balance. This is much like our internal gyroscope or our vestibular equilibrium system that God has for us called the person of The Holy Spirit.

CHAPTER FIVE
GOD'S COMMUNICATION SYSTEM

For the past two chapters we have seen how we were created to speak and hear and communicate physically. Now we will see how we were created to speak and hear the Word of God with interpersonal communication with the Creator of the Universe.

Over the years I have taught about what is being written in this book. This board is just one of the incarnations of these thoughts. Some have accused me of writing in tongues, and they are not too far off from the truth. If only I could get an interpretation.

Remember, when we started this book, we talked about the make-up of mankind. We are spirit, soul and body that interact with other beings on planet Earth who are also spirit, soul and body. This communication process of speaking and hearing the Word of God is where we hear God speak and where we either communicate back to God or we communicate with other humans. To communicate with other humans we both need to have a sender and receiving system. This would be our voice and our ears. Each one has a set within them. What coordinates this system is our brains that encodes information and then decodes this information and returns transmission.

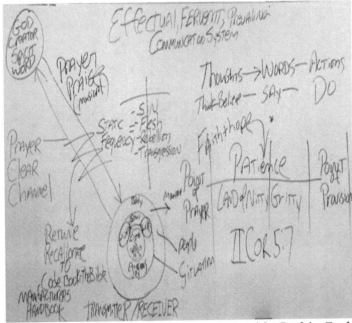

Our communication system to interact with God is God-given because—from the beginning—God wanted to communicate, interact and have fellowship with man and woman. God communicates via His Spirit to our human spirit. This communication system is not based on wisdom of man or the power of man, but is based on the power of Spirit, God and faith.

POWER: Dunamis (doo'-nam-is)=From G1410; force (literally or figuratively); specifically miraculous power (usually by implication a miracle itself): - ability, abundance, meaning, might (-ily, -y, -y deed), (worker of) miracle (-s), power, strength, violence, mighty (wonderful) work. G1410: dunamai (doo'-nam-ahee)=Of uncertain affinity; to be able or possible: - be able, can (do, + -not), could, may, might, be possible, be of power. (*Strong's*)

Paul states that he had a message, that he preached and spoke and it was not based on earthly wisdom.

> *"And when I came to you, brethren, I did not come with superiority of speech or of wisdom, proclaiming to you the testimony of God."*

I Corinthians 2:1

Paul had heard a Word from God and was speaking what he had heard to human beings to hear.

> *"And my message **(word)** and my preaching **(of the Word)** were not in persuasive words of wisdom, but in demonstration of the Spirit and of power, that your faith should not rest on the wisdom of men, but on the power of God."*

I Corinthians 2:4-5 (emphasis mine)

Paul stated that speaking God's wisdom is a mystery, a hidden wisdom. (I Corinthians 2:8)

> *"But just as it is written, 'Things which eye has not seen and ear has not heard and which has not entered the heart of man, all that God has prepared for those who love Him.'"*

I Corinthians 2:9

So God is speaking and Paul is speaking God's wisdom. Now we are beginning to see how to hear and speak the things of the Lord, and the hardware that God has created within us.

The good news is that God has prepared mysteries to be

revealed to us, the ones that He loves. God's heartbeat is communication of revealed mysteries. He has thoughts to communicate. God is the Reveler of mysteries.

> *"For to us God revealed them through the Spirit; for the Spirit searches all things even the depths of God."*
>
> I Corinthians 2:10

We have mentioned before that words are nothing but breath-driven thoughts and God's Words are Spirit-driven (ruach/pneuma/breath) thoughts. God's desire is to be the Revealer as the Holy Spirit is the Searcher Who searches the depths of God, where God's deepest thoughts reside. The Holy Spirit not only is the Searcher but also the conduit through Whom God reveals his mysteries.

> *"For who among men knows the thoughts of a man except the spirit* **(little s)** *of the man, which is in him* **(location of the little s)***? Even so the thoughts of God no one knows except the Spirit* **(Big S)** *of God."*
>
> I Corinthians 2:11 (emphasis mine)

Men have thoughts. So do wo-men. For that matter all hu-mans have thoughts and, unless they reveal those thoughts, no one will really know what they are thinking. Unless they communicate their thoughts, those thoughts will remain secret or a mystery. God's communication system, between the Creator and the created is *Big S* to the *little s*. The Holy Spirit Who searches the depths of God for the thoughts of God connects with our *little s* (human spirit) and reveals the thoughts of God to us.

Now some may be wondering that if God is revealing mysteries, then why am I so limited in what I know about God? This is why I have my go-to verse when I just don't know something about God. Some call it my cop-out verse, but it sure helps me when I don't understand all I think I know about God. There is purpose in His communicative revelations to us. The purpose is to obey and do to fulfill His purposes in our (and others') lives.

> *"The secret things belong to the Lord our God, but the things revealed belong to us and to our sons forever, that we may observe* ***(do)*** *all the words of this law."*
>
> Deuteronomy 29:29 (emphasis mine)

> *"The person who has My commands and keeps them is the one who [really] loves Me, and whoever [really] loves Me will be loved by My Father, and I [too] will love him and will show (reveal, manifest) Myself to him—I will let Myself be clearly seen by him and make Myself real to him."*
>
> John 14:21
> The Amplified Bible

The New American Standard Version of John 14:21 uses the word "disclose" for the word "show." If we desire to have disclosure, revelation and manifestation of Jesus, it is all hinged on love and obedience.

It is this love and obedience that opens up the lines of communication and removes the static and gets us on the right frequency to hear the voice of God clearly.

> *"Now we have received, not the spirit of the world, but the Spirit who is from God, that we might know the things freely given us by God."*
>
> I Corinthians 2:12

The "spirit of the world" is not the "Spirit Who is from God." This thing called the "spirit of the world" is an attitude undergirded by satanic influences. The d-evil (little *d*) is known as "the prince of the power of the air" and is a spirit that is working in the sons of disobedience. It is a course or a systematic working in human beings.

> *"And you were dead in your trespasses and sins, in which you formerly walked according to the course of this world, according to the prince of the power of the air, of the spirit that is now working in the sons of disobedience."*
>
> Ephesians 2:1-2

We also see that "the god of this world" has blinded people's minds so they cannot see the "light of the gospel."

> *"And even if our gospel is veiled, it is veiled to those who are perishing, in whose case the god of this world has blinded the minds of the unbelieving, that they might not see the light of the gospel of the glory of Christ, who is the image of God."*
>
> II Corinthians 4:3-4

The prince of the power of the air—the god of this world—gives static to our communication system so we cannot hear or perceive the Word of God as He speaks to us.

When we are influenced by "the spirit of this world" in our receiving mechanism (our spirits), we are unable to, "know 'the things freely given to us by God.'" Of course these things freely given to us are,

> *"…things which eye has not seen and ear has not heard, and which have not entered the heart of man, all that God has prepared for those who love Him."*
>
> I Corinthians 2:9

Remember that we have been created to communicate with God and one another. In the physical realm we have a sound generator (vocal folds) that sends forth sound waves (vibrations) through our body and as our articulators (lips, tongue, etc.) forms the thoughts and we speak our mind. Those breath-formed thoughts travel through the air to someone who has a receiver and they receive those words via the acoustic system (our ears) and those words are decoded so they will make sense. All humans have a sending and receiving system (vocal cords, ears) and all humans have a decoding/encoding system (the brain). So communication is a constant exchange of thoughts as we speak and hear, and hear and speak. Whether we heard each other is the crux of communication problems in the world today.

Our Spiritual Communication System (S.C.S) is set up in a similar fashion. God is the originator of the system and has everything He needs. He is omnipresent, omniscience, and omnipotent, so He is not limited by poor positioning, distance and ability to hear us. If there are communication difficulties, it is not on God's part but on our end. The old saying is "If you can't find God, He did not move, but you did." If there is frequency difficulties, static or even no communication, we may need to deal with sin and repent, or exercise our authority and tell the d-evil (little *d*), to begone, get out, scat!

So we have our receiver (our human spirit) and our sound generator (our mouths) and our decoder and encoder system (our brains). One thing that we must do with our S.C.S. is to keep it calibrated. We must keep the frequency tuned to God's channel, and remove the static of the world system (under the control of the d-evil as the god of this world). We must have our encoder and decoder fine-tuned and we must have our code book (the Bible, aka

The Manufacturer's Handbook) so that we may know what God is saying. This is where we must renew our minds so that we will be thinking like God thinks. If we don't renew our minds, we will default to thinking in the flesh and—even worse—thinking like and coming into agreement with the d-evil.

CHAPTER SIX
THE TWISTED LANGUAGE

According to the book, *Terminology of Communicative Disorders Speech-Language-Hearing Third Edition* by Lucille Nicolosi, Elizabeth Harryman and Janet Kresheck, "language" is:

"Any accepted, structure, symbolic system for interpersonal communication composed of sounds arranged in ordered sequence to form words, with rules for combining these words into sequence or strings that express thoughts, intentions, experiences, and feelings; comprised of phonological, morphological, syntactical and semantic components."

If we boil that definition down to the bottom line, language is an agreed upon code to express thoughts. For example, if you see a book—much like the one that you are holding in your hand right now—and set it down on a table and then sit in a chair, we have come into agreement on certain things. We agree that the thing with a cover, words written inside and has a spine is called "a book." It is sitting on a flat surface that is held up with legs, called "a table." And the thing you are sitting on with a seat and a back and legs is called "a chair." The confusion would arise, if you called the thing with a cover, words written inside and with a spine "a chair." There may be different words in other languages for those items, but the bottom line, in any language there is an agreed upon code for what we call the book, table and chair. Imagine the chaos and confusion if the languages were not agreed upon. Words would be useless for the purpose of communication. Of course communication can be more than just words to express thoughts. A glance, body posture, facial expressions all speak louder than words sometimes; especially hidden thoughts that we try to mask.

As with our natural language, where there are things that cause problems in growth and development, so it is with our spiritual language for hearing and speaking the Word of God. This is where there is static and confusion as we not only try to hear and speak, but actually try to obey Him. If you can't understand Him, you will never be able to obey Him.

THE LANGUAGE OF CONFUSION

At one point in time, the whole earth used the same language and the same words. In the margin of my Bible corresponding to Genesis 11:1, it reads like this;

"Now the whole earth was one lip and one set of words."

Genesis 11:1

The survivors of the flood, the descendants of Noah and his sons Shem, Ham, and Japheth and their families, journeyed and found a plain in the land of Shinar and settled there. (Genesis 11:2)

Once settled, they, "said to one another" since they used the same language and the same words,

"Come, let us make bricks and burn them thoroughly."

And then they said,

"Come let us build for ourselves a city, and a tower (a ziggurat) whose top will reach into heaven, and let us make for ourselves a name, lest we be scattered abroad over the face of the whole earth."

(Genesis 11:3-4)

Notice that they were using man-made bricks (unnatural) for stone (natural) and tar for mortar.

These people had an *agreed upon code* used to communicate their desires for "ourselves." Notice that it was not, "let us build a city for God or make a name for God," but for "ourselves." Their fear was being "scattered abroad."

The Lord came down and checked out what they had built for themselves and made the observation:

"And the Lord said, 'Behold, they are one people, and they all have the same language. And this is what they began to do, and now nothing which they purpose to do will be impossible for them.'"

Genesis 11:6

It looks like the Lord knew that they were a danger to their own selves. It reminds me of Adam and Eve after they committed high treason with disobedience and brought the curse on themselves and on the whole world. (Read Genesis 3:1-24 for full details of the fall). The Lord expelled them from the Garden and set cherubim holding the flaming sword which turned in every direction, to

43

guard the way to the Tree of Life. If they had got back to the Tree of Life, they would live forever under a curse. So it is with God's next move to save mankind from themselves and their one language and same words.

NOTE: It is a little known fact that this Genesis 3 passage is the first mention of a car in the Bible.

> *"So he drove the man out…"*
>
> Genesis 3:24

Later on we see that there was also mentioned a 120 seat Honda mentioned in the Bible, when on the day of Pentecost, "they were all in one accord…" (Acts 2:1)

NOTE TO THE NOTE: I would apologize for those last two comments about cars in the Bible, but I am not really sorry. It strikes me as being funny.

> *"Come, let Us go down and there confuse their language, that they may not understand one another's speech one lip."*
>
> Genesis 11:7

NOTE: When we get to the chapter on Speaking In Tongues, we will talk about God not being the "author of confusion." (This is aka *a teaser.*)

So, God being good to His Word came down and scattered the people abroad over the face of the earth. The cause-and-effect of this scattering was, they stopped building the city for themselves. (Genesis 11:8) The name of the city was called Babel (*Bay-bull* not *Baa-bull*) because,

> *"…the Lord confused the language of the whole earth; and from there the Lord scattered them abroad over the face of the whole earth."*
>
> Genesis 11:9

Isn't it ironic that the very thing that the people did not want to happen happened? They were scattered. This speaks to me, of my own plans at times, where I conferred with other people and forged ahead with building monuments to myself, and I found that I would get confused, disoriented, scattered and begin to speak nonsense.

THE ADAM AND EVE CONNECTION

We have seen in Chapter One that we are fearfully and wonderfully made and we are part of the creative process by the Creator. We saw that God used Himself as the blueprint and the Master Design, as Adam and Eve were designed by The Master. We also saw how God took a lump of clay and breathed His breath into this lump of clay's nostrils, and the clay became a living being/soul. It bears repeating;

"We are nothing but lumps of clay filled with the breath of God." (Bruce Coble)

The first indication that God communicated with this new creation, was found in Genesis 2:16.

> *"And the Lord God commanded the man, saying, 'From any tree of the Garden you may eat freely; but from the tree of the knowledge of good and evil you shall not eat, for in the day you eat, you shall surely die.'"*

> Genesis 2:16-17

Apparently, at this point, God spoke a language, that Adam understood. Some have theorized that spoken words were not used, but telepathic thought waves where God thought it, and Adam perceived those thoughts and understood. I have no real problem about that theory, but as a Speech-Language Pathologist, I like the idea of God commanding and saying words in creation of the world, and in communication with His creation. After all the Genesis account says,

> *"Then God **said... (not just thought)**..."*
>
> Genesis 1:3 (emphasis mine)

God continued communication with His creation, this time in reference to Adam being alone.

> *"Then the Lord God said, it is not good for the man to be alone, I will make him a helper suitable for him."*
>
> Genesis 2:18

At this point, the Lord had the first anesthesia administered and the first surgical removal of a rib, and the first surgical closure, and the first fashion show and the first time a father walked His girl down the aisle for the first marriage.

> *"So the Lord God caused a deep sleep to fall upon the man, and he slept; then He took one of the ribs, and closed up the flesh in that place. And the Lord fashioned into a woman the rib which He had taken from the man, and brought her to the man. And the man, said, 'This is now bone of my bones, and flesh of my flesh; She shall be called Woman, because she was taken out of Man.' For this cause a man shall leave his father and his mother, and shall cleave to his wife; and they shall become one flesh. And the man and his wife were both naked and were not ashamed."*
>
> Genesis 2:21-25

The story now shifts to the Language of Lies.

THE LANGUAGE OF LIES (Enter the Serpent)

In the early 70's, there was a movie starring Bruce Lee called *Enter the Dragon*. It was the premier karate movie of the time, propelling Bruce Lee to stardom. As we look at Genesis 3 we could call this section 'Enter the Serpent.'

> *"Now the serpent (little s) was more crafty than any beast of the field which the Lord God had made…"*

Genesis 3:1

Just who is this serpent (little *s*) who was a created being? Well, according to Revelation 20:2-3,

> *"And he (an angel) laid hold of the dragon, the serpent of old, who is the **d-evil** and Satan, and bound him for a thousand years, and threw him into the abyss, and shut it and sealed it over him, so that he should not deceive the nations any longer, until the thousand years were completed; after these things he must be released for a short time."*

Revelation 20:2-3 (emphasis mine)

This serpent, the d-evil (little *d*), satan (little *s*), was a deceiver, which we will see taking place in Genesis 3. As the serpent entered the Garden, he entered with lies on his lips. A lie is defined as:

LIE: Pseudos (psyoo'-dos)=From G5574; a falsehood: - lie, lying. G5574: pseudomai (psyoo'-dom-ahee)=Middle voice of an apparently primary verb; to utter an untruth or attempt to deceive by falsehood: - falsely, lie. (*Strong's*)

Dictionary.com defines a lie as:

- A false statement made with deliberate intent to deceive; an intentional untruth; a falsehood

- Something intended or serving to convey a false impression; imposture
- An inaccurate or false statement; a falsehood
- The charge or accusation of telling a lie
- To speak falsely or utter untruth knowingly, as with intent to deceive
- To express what is false; convey a false impression

This defines the serpent and his ways with Eve. Let's check out how Jesus defines the d-evil and his ilk.

*"You are of your father the d-evil, and you want to do the desires of your father. He **(the d-evil)** was a murderer from the beginning, and does not stand in the truth, because there is no truth in him. Whenever he speaks a lie, he speaks from his own nature; for he is a liar, and the father of lies."*

John 8:44 (emphasis mine)

When the d-evil speaks from his own nature, he lies; when Jesus speaks from His own nature, He speaks truth. When Jesus speaks, He only speaks what the Father speaks, so Father God is a Truth Speaker.

Let's check out how the serpent deceived the woman, along with the man. Let's check out his L.M.O. (Lying Modus Operandi).

"...And he said to the woman, 'Indeed, has God said, you shall not eat from any tree of the Garden?'"

Genesis 3:1

The nature of a lie is that it is a perversion of the truth. Just a little poison in a glass of water will make the whole glass poisonous, so it is with a lie. There may be just enough of the Word of God mixed in with a twisted lie to pervert the thing.

The first thing the serpent did was to cast doubt on what God had spoken. "Indeed, has God said…" (Genesis 3:1) Well the answer was yes, (*Indeed*) He has. She affirmed to the serpent, "…God has said you shall not eat from it or touch it, lest you die." The serpent continues with his lies by putting into her mind that God was mistaken when He said, "You surely shall not die." (Genesis 3:4) He then puts into doubt about God's motives, "For God knows that in the day you eat from it your eyes will be opened and you will be like God, knowing good and evil." (Genesis 3:5)

At that point, the woman fell into the trap the L.L.P. syndrome (1) The Lust of the flesh (2) the Lust of the eyes (3) the boastful Pride of life. The d-evil has nothing new under the sun and will use these same temptations on Jesus and later on to the Church at large. (See Matthew 4 and Luke 4 for details)

> "*For all that is in the world, the lust of the flesh and the lust of the eyes and the boastful pride of life, is not from the Father, but is from the world.*"
>
> I John 2:16

At the point of disobedience, not only had the serpent entered the Garden, but also the curse. We all have experienced this curse and fall because of *words*. Adam and Eve chose to believe the words and lies of the d-evil as opposed to the Words of Life from the Father. The cause-and-effect is death. That is why it is so important for us to know and hear and speak and obey the Word of God.

THE BATTLE OF WORDS (Truth versus Lie)

We have mentioned the satanic, d-evilish temptation of Jesus in the Wilderness. This was a battle of words. This was a battle between the lie and the truth.

NOTE: Most people's concept about temptation (being tempted) is to be enticed into some kind of gross sin or destructive habit. The best definition of temptation that I have heard was from a Larry Napier, a Bible teacher and friend of mine. In a teaching on spiritual warfare, he said that "Temptation is not designed necessarily to pull you into something but to pull you away from who you are and your destiny." Larry told me once, "It is not the non-Christian who is tempted, but the Christian. The non-believer is deceived already and does not need to be tempted; he is already trapped."

Jesus had just come out a very uplifting experience. He had been baptized in the Jordan River by John the *Dipper* (Baptizer) and the heavens were opened, the Spirit of God (in the shape of a dove) came down and stayed upon Him, and spoken words of affirmation were spoken by the Father.

> "...*this is My beloved Son in whom I am well-pleased.*"
> Matthew 3:17; Luke 3:22

The d-evil was trying to put some static on the connection between the Father and the Son. Like the serpent in the Garden, the d-evil was trying to entice Jesus away from His mission, purpose and destiny.

> "*The one who practices sin is of the* **d-evil***; for the devil has sinned from the beginning. The Son of God appeared for this purpose, that He might destroy the works of the* **d-evil.**"
> I John 3:8 (emphasis mine)

Is it any wonder that the d-evil would attempt to pull Jesus away from His purpose? Solomon says, "...so, there is nothing new under the sun..." (Ecclesiastes 1:9) and this is true with Adam and Eve, Jesus, followers of Jesus and yes, even now for you and me. The d-evil/serpent used lying, twisted words in the Garden, he used lying twisted words on Jesus and he uses lying twisted words on us.

This is a picture from our trip to Israel of the wilderness, the site of the temptation of Jesus. It is vast, dry, desolate, and where the d-evil attempted to pull Jesus away from His purpose.

"Then Jesus was led up by the Spirit into the wilderness to be tempted by the d-evil."

Matthew 4:1

"And Jesus, full of the Spirit, returned from the Jordan and was led about by the Spirit in the wilderness."

Luke 4:1

It needs to be understood that, in the midst of the

temptation, Jesus was full of the Spirit and was led about in the wilderness by the Spirit. The temptation came at the point of hunger after Jesus had fasted for forty days and forty nights. (Luke 4:1-2; Matthew 4:1-2) At this point, "And the d-evil said to Him…" (Luke 4:3) Matthew's account puts it this way, "And the tempter came and said to Him…" (Matthew 4:3) So this is how it went down:

The Spirit of God came upon Jesus.

The Father spoke words of affirmation of pleasure in the Son.

Jesus was led by the Spirit of God to, and about, the wilderness.

The d-evil, the tempter, came to Jesus and started a conversation as he spoke words to Him.

The d-evil began by putting doubt into Who He (Jesus) was by throwing down the "if" card, just like he had done with Eve.

"If you are the Son of God, command that these stones become bread."

Matthew 4:3

The first point of temptation is for Jesus to use His words of authority for a miracle to meet His own need, bread for hunger.

Jesus counters this temptation to use His words, by quoting the written Word, Deuteronomy 8:3.

"But He answered and said, it is written, man shall not live by bread alone, but on every word that proceeds out of the mouth of God."

Matthew 4:4; Luke 4:4; Deuteronomy 8:3

In the New American Standard Bible, it says it in a little more speech-oriented way.

> "...*man does not live by bread alone, but man lives by everything that proceeds out of the mouth of the Lord.*"
>
> Deuteronomy 8:3

I like the phrase, "...everything that proceeds *out of the mouth* of the Lord." As we have spoken about previously, when we speak words—speak our thoughts—they are driven by breath. When God speaks, the "everything" that proceeds out of His mouth is "Spirit" and "Words." It is Spirit-driven God Thoughts and Words that we live by.

The next point of enticement/temptation starts with the d-evil speaking more doubt into what Jesus was.

> "*Then the* **d-evil** *took Him into the holy city; and he stood Him on the pinnacle of the temple, and said to Him, 'If you are the Son of God, throw Yourself down; for it is written...'*"
>
> Matthew 4:5-6 (emphasis mine)

The d-evil saw that Jesus was going to use the Word of God, so he decided to twist the Word for his purposes.

> "*...for it is written, 'He will give His angels charge concerning You; and on their hands they will bear You up, lest You strike Your foot against a stone.'*"
>
> Matthew 4:6, Psalm 91:11-12

> "*Jesus said to him, 'On the other hand, it is written you shall not tempt the Lord your God.'*"
>
> Matthew 4:7, Deuteronomy 6:16

The next level of temptation was when the d-evil took Jesus to a very high mountain, and showed Him all the kingdoms of the world, and their glory; and said to Him:

"All these things will I give You, if You fall down and worship me."

Matthew 4:8

At this point in the interpersonal communication interaction between Jesus and the d-evil, Jesus spoke to the d-evil with a word of authority when He said:

"Begone, Satan. For it is written, 'You shall worship the Lord your God, and serve Him only.'"

Matthew 4:10

As this battle ends, the d-evil left Him. (Matthew 4:11) The Luke passage puts it this way:

"And when the d-evil had finished every temptation, he departed from Him until an opportune time."

Luke 4:13

NOTE: Jesus entered this wilderness experience full of the Spirit, was led about by the Spirit and returned to Galilee in the power of the Spirit. (Matthew 4:1; Luke 4:1; Luke 4:14) As we face temptation in our own personal wilderness experience, we can come out the other side if we rely on the Spirit, speak the Word/Truth and exercise the authority given by God to His followers. The cause-and-effect of Jesus going through this battle of The Word (God truth) versus the word (d-evil lies) is found in the passage at Hebrews that contains insight into the *Sword of the Spirit*, The Word of God (Hebrews 4:12). We will look later at the Hebrews 4:12 passage, but the context of the temptation is linked to it.

"For we do not have a high priest who cannot sympathize with our weaknesses, but one who has been tempted in all

things as we are, yet without sin. Let us therefore draw near with confidence to the throne of grace, that we may receive mercy and may find grace to help in time of need."

Hebrews 4:15-16

CHAPTER SEVEN
THE POWER OF THE WORD

"Sticks and stones may break my bones, but words can never harm me." (*The Christian Recorder* March 1862)

"You think that I don't even mean a single word I say. It's only words and words are all I have, to take your heart away." (The Bee Gees)

"Sanctify them by truth, Thy Word is truth."
-Jesus; John 17:17

Words are merely expressed thoughts. The expression can be verbal or non-verbal. They can be thought, spoken, written or by finger movements (various sign languages). The meaning and intent of words can be enhanced by facial expression or vocal intonation, prosody and intensity. The book, *Terminology of Communication Disorders* by Lucille Nicolosi, Elizabeth Harryman, and Janet Kresheck defines "word" as:

"A free form consisting of one or more phonemes (speech sounds) and one or more syllables (vowel/consonant) which has meaning without being divisible into smaller units capable of independent use."

Words, when put in the context of a sentence, become part of our language structure. As stated earlier, language is an agreed upon code by which we communicate. The usage of words in language have rules by which we judge words as we connect them sequentially "to express our thoughts, intentions, experiences and feelings." (*Terminology of Communication Disorders*). These rules include:

- Semantics (word meaning)
- Syntax (word order)
- Pragmatics (word usage/intent)
- Phonological (sound production)
- Morphological (smallest meaningful unit of sound)

The combination of all of these areas forms the language of our world of words.

As we have mentioned before, that this world was created in the beginning by the spoken word by God.

JESUS THE WORD (The Logos)

"In the beginning was the Word, and the Word was with God and the Word was God."

John 1:1

WORD: Logos (log'-os)=From G3004; something said (including the thought); by implication a topic (subject of discourse), also reasoning (the mental faculty) or motive; by extension a computation; specifically (with the article in John) the Divine Expression (that is, Christ): - account, cause, communication, X concerning, doctrine, fame, X have to do, intent, matter, mouth, preaching, question, reason, + reckon, remove, say (-ing), shew, X speaker, speech, talk, thing, + none of these things move me, tidings, treatise, utterance, word, work. G3004: lego (leg'-o)=A primary verb; properly to "lay" forth, that is, (figuratively) relate (in words [usually of systematic or set discourse; whereas G2036 and G5346 generally refer to an individual expression or speech respectively; while G4483 is properly to break silence merely, and G2980 means an extended or random harangue]); by implication to mean: - ask, bid, boast, call, describe, give out, name, put forth, say (-ing, on), shew, speak, tell, utter. (*Strong's*)

As we look at the John passage about "the Word" we will see that this "Word" is, in reality, Jesus. When you realize that Jesus is "The Word," then you can logically place the name "Jesus" in place of the word, "Word" and not change the meaning of the passage, but enhance and clarify the meaning.

> "*In the beginning was Jesus, and Jesus was with God, and Jesus was God.*"
>
> John 1:1

> "*In the beginning was the Logos, and the Logos was with God, and the Logos was God.*"
>
> John 1:1

This view of Jesus elevates Him above the thought that He was a good man, a teacher or a prophet. He is more than just some kid that was born in Bethlehem who grew up in Nazareth, and became some kind of religious nut. C.S. Lewis wrote about the perspective of Who Jesus is and what we cannot assume about the Word.

"I am trying here to prevent anyone saying the really foolish thing that people often say about Him: I'm ready to accept Jesus as a great moral teacher, but I don't accept his claim to be God. That is the one thing we must not say. A man who was merely a man and said the sort of things Jesus said would not be a great moral teacher. He would either be a lunatic—on the level with the man who says he is a poached egg—or else he would be the Devil of Hell. You must make your choice. Either this man was, and is, the Son of God, or else a madman or something worse. You can shut him up for a fool, you can spit at him and kill him as a demon or you can fall at his feet and call him Lord and God, but let us not come with any patronizing nonsense about his being a great human teacher. He has not left that open to us. He did not intend to." (C.S. Lewis; *Mere Christianity*)

The question that arises for you, if you are reading this book, is Who do you say that Jesus is? The word meaning that you give to Jesus determines the pragmatics of how you respond and express yourself about Him.

JOHN 1:1-14 (Jesus: The Logos Word)

I like to write out John 1:1-14 placing Jesus in the place of the word, "Word." It gives me insight into Who He is to me and to the world.

> *In the beginning was Jesus*
> *And Jesus was with God*
> *And Jesus was God*
> *Jesus was in the beginning with God*
> *All things came into being through Jesus*
> *And apart from Jesus nothing came into being that has come into being*
> *In Jesus was life* **(radiance of God's glory)***; and the life* **(radiance of God's glory)** *was the light of men*
> *And the light* **(radiance of God's glory**) *shines in the darkness and the darkness did not comprehend* **(overpower it)**

There came a man **(John the Baptist/Dipper)** *from God, whose name was John*

He **(John)** *came for a witness, that he might bear witness of the light, that all might believe through him*

He **(John)** *was not the true light, but came that he might bear witness of the light*

There was a true light which, coming into the world enlightens every man

Jesus was in the world, and the world was made through Jesus, and the world did not know Jesus

Jesus came to His own, and those who were Jesus' own did not receive Jesus

But as many as received Jesus, to them Jesus gave the right **(exousia/delegated authority)** *to become children of God, even to those who believe (trust in, cling to, rely on) in Jesus' name*

Who were not born of blood **(physical birth)** *nor of the will of the flesh* **(an act of our will)**, *but of God*

And Jesus became flesh **(incarnated)**, *and dwelt among us* **(for 33 years)** *and we beheld Jesus' glory as of the only begotten from the Father, full of grace and truth."*

(emphasis mine)

This same Jesus/The Word/The Logos was the verbal expression of the thoughts of the Father. God used "prophets in many portions and in many ways" to speak to the fathers. God spoke the Word "in His Son."

"God, after he spoke long ago to the fathers in the prophets in many portions and in many ways, in these last days has spoken to us in His Son **(Jesus/The Word/The Logos)**, *whom He* **(the Father)** *appointed heir of all things, through whom also He made the world."*

Hebrews 1:1-2 (emphasis mine)

This involvement in creation is underscored by Paul in his letter to the church at Colossae.

> "For He **(the Father)** *delivered us from the domain* **(authority)** *of darkness, and transferred us to the kingdom of His beloved Son* **(Jesus/The Word/The Logos)**, *in whom we have redemption, the forgiveness of sins. And He* **(Jesus/The Word/The Logos)** *is the image of the invisible God, the first-borne of all creation. For in Him* **(Jesus/The Word/The Logos)** *all things were created, both in the heavens and on earth, visible and invisible, whether thrones or dominions or rulers or authorities—all things have been created through Him and for Him. And He* **(Jesus/The Word/The Logos)** *is before all things, and in Him all things come together."*
>
> Colossians 1:13-17 (emphasis mine)

Paul again underscores this thought line in his letter of correction to the Church of God in Corinth.

> "For even if there are so-called gods **(little g)** *whether in heaven or on earth, as indeed there are many gods and many lords, whom are all things, and we exist for Him* **(the Father)**, *from whom are all things, and we exist for Him; and one Lord Jesus Christ* **(the Word/the Logos)**, *through whom we are all things, an d we exist through Him."*
>
> I Corinthians 8:5-6 (emphasis mine)

These verses drives the point home to me that when God was in the process of creation, Jesus was there, the Holy Spirit was there and the Father was there.

> "In the beginning God created the heavens and the earth. And the earth was formless and void, and darkness was over the surface of the deep, and the Spirit of God was moving

over the surface of the waters. Then God said **(spoke the Word)...**"

Genesis 1:1-3 (emphasis mine)

Also at the point of creation of man/woman (as distinct from animals), the "Us" and "Our" that is spoken of, becomes clear as to Who They were.

"Then God said, Let Us make man in Our image according to Our likeness..."

Genesis 1:26

Hey, I could be wrong, but the "Us" and "Our" that was used as the blueprint and divine design, seems to be (1) The Father (2) The Son/Jesus/The Word/The Logos (3) The Holy Spirit.

THE WRITTEN WORD

God's thoughts expressed in any form are life. For some reason, He has allowed His thoughts to be expressed in the written form called the Bible. In the next chapter we will look at the Logos-Rhema Connection of the Word where the Logos is the universal Word to humanity and the Rhema becomes more strategic to the individual.

Let's look at the written Word.

THE FOREVER WORD

"The grass withers, the flower fades, but the Word of our God shall stand forever."

Isaiah 40:8

Words of human beings seems to have longevity, as we look at authors, poets, musicians, actors and even memories of what people have said to us, but compared to The Word of God the longevity of human words tends to come up short. To quote a song by Glass Harp, "never is a long, long, long, long time." Forever speaks of a fresh, growing, ever brilliant, non-fading word. To quote another singer by the name of Buddy Holly, "Not fade away." This means that the Word of God will stand the test of time. Fads will come and go, people come in and out of our lives, powers will rise and fall; but the one thing in life that will not change is the Word of God.

THE SURGICAL SWORD

> *"For the Word of God is living and active and sharper than any two-edged sword, and piercing as far as the divisions of soul and spirit, of both joints and marrow, and able to judge the thoughts and intentions of the heart."*

Hebrews 4:12

A sword that is dull and rarely used is more of an artifact than a weapon. A sword placed on display is wonderful to look at, think about and even be proud of, but unless the sword is sharpened and used, it is ineffective in our lives.

The Sword of the Word of God is alive, breathing, useful and ready at any time when a need arises. It is sharp, honed in the fires of God and does not lose its edge. As far as the human eye can perceive, there is no division between the soul and spirit, joint and marrow, thoughts and intentions; but when the living, active, sharp two-edge sword of the Word of God is used by the Great Physician, there is nothing but surgical precision. This living Word is living and active because of God breath, as when God breathed His breath into a lump of clay in the Garden, and the lump of clay became a living soul.

THE TEACHING WORD

*"All Scripture is inspired **(God breathed)** by God and profitable for teaching, for reproof, for correction, for training in righteousness, that the man of God may be adequate, equipped for every good work."*

II Timothy 3:16-17 (emphasis mine)

There is a big difference in an employee who is inadequate and poorly equipped and the employee who is adequately equipped for the job at hand. It will be the difference between a good work and a good work gone bad.

The way that the Word in Hebrews 4:12 became living and active is found in II Timothy 3:16-17. It is the same way that an inanimate and non-active lump of clay became living and activated. It is the breath and inspiration of God. Once Adam had God breath blown into his nostrils, and he became alive, God placed him in the Garden for purpose. So it is with our relation to this God breathed and inspired Word, so that we can get on with a good work or purpose. Our lives, the world that we live in now, our Garden. Don't think for a minute that the serpent won't try to crawl in and deceive us. That is why we need this profitable Word. I believe it would behoove us to break down this verse to see how this Word becomes our teacher under the tutelage of the Holy Spirit.

NOTE: In my educational experience, I became certified to teach kindergarten through twelfth grade which included student teaching. I never taught in the school system, but chose to practice on the adult level in the medical field. I also received my Masters in Education with an emphasis on Speech. I have also taught the Bible in the Ruminator Sunday School class for 25 plus years. I relate this information not to brag on my credentials, but to say I see the validity of the way the Word is used in teaching and how I have taught over the years. With that said, let's break down this verse.

ALL: Pas (pas)=Including all the forms of declension; apparently a primary word; all, any, every, the whole: - all (manner of, means) alway (-s), any (one), X daily, + ever, every (one, way), as many as, + no (-thing), X thoroughly, whatsoever, whole, whosoever. (*Strong's*)

SCRIPTURE: graphe (graf-ay')=From G1125; a document, that is, holy Writ (or its contents or a statement in it): - scripture. G1125: grapho (graf'-o)=A primary verb; to "grave," especially to write; figuratively to describe: - describe, write (-ing, -ten). (*Strong's*)

NOTE: At the time of the writing of this verse, there was not a New Testament, so the "all Scripture" referred to was the Old Testament writings. These writings were God's revelation to mankind about Himself. Later, the New Testament was written and include in the Scriptures.

NOTE TO THE NOTE: I am convinced that you cannot expect to understand the New Testament (The skinny part of the Book) unless you understand the Old Testament (The fat part of the Book).

NOTE TO THE NOTE TO THE NOTE: I like the way Smith Wigglesworth stated it, "Some people like to read the Bible in the Hebrew, some like to read it in the Greek, I like to read it in the Holy Spirit." For more information about how the Scriptures came into being, check out the books, *Evidence That Demands a Verdict* by Josh McDowell and *What The Bible Is All About* by Henrietta Mears.

GOD BREATHED: Theopneustos (theh-op'-nyoo-stos)=From G2316 and a presumed derivative of G4154; divinely breathed in: - given by inspiration of God. G2316: theos (theh'-os)=Of uncertain affinity; a deity, especially (with G3588) the supreme Divinity; figuratively a magistrate; by Hebraism very: - X exceeding, God, god [-ly, -ward]. (*Strong's*)

NOTE: These writings are not from the imaginations of men and women; they are thoughts from the Creator of the Universe that were spoken thoughts fueled by the Spirit of God. These Spirited-breathed Words are, like we pointed out in the Hebrews 4:12 passage, made alive like a lump of clay in the Garden when God breathed His breath (inspiration) and the lump of clay became a living soul.

PROFITABLE: o phelimos (o-fel'-ee-mos)=helpful or serviceable, that is, advantageous: - profit (-able). (*Strong's*)

NOTE: The great works of authors throughout the years has been beneficial for many things. They have been beneficial for enjoyment, for encouragement, for provoking thought, for social change (good, bad, and ugly), for entertainment, for many reasons. But the God-breathed Scriptures is profitable for revelation, lives changed for the better, encouragement, challenge that will be forever. There is a reason that for years, this collection of 66 books bound in leather has been on the best sellers list.

TEACHING: Didaskalia (did-as-kal-ee'-ah)=From G1320; instruction (the function or the information): - doctrine, learning, teaching. G1320: didaskalos (did-as'-kal-os)=From G1321; an instructor (generally or specifically): - doctor, master, teacher. G1321: didasko (did-as'-ko)=A prolonged (causative) form of a primary verb δα□ω dao (to learn); to teach (in the same broad application): - teach. (*Strong's*)

NOTE: The Scriptures are our touchstone for the truth, the standard by which we measure all words. When the teacher teaches, it must be more than just our opinions to pontificate about, but to point to the truth. Then the Holy Spirit, who is the Teacher, will lead us into all truth. As a teacher, I have learned that this part of the profit of the Word is the presentation of the Word. What we do with it is entirely up to us. The old saying goes, "You can lead a horse (or cow) to water, but you can't make them drink."

REPROOF: Elegchos (el'-eng-khos)=From G1651; proof, conviction: - evidence, reproof. G1651: elegcho (el-eng'-kho)=Of uncertain affinity; to confute, admonish: - convict, convince, tell a fault, rebuke, reprove. (*Strong's*)

NOTE: After the presentation of truth or the teaching in a school setting, there will be a proving of what you have been taught. This is called a test. Of course, we know that when you stand in faith, there will be a testing of your faith; so it is with when you are taught the Word.

CORRECTION: epanortho sis (ep-an-or'-tho-sis)= a straightening up again, that is, (figuratively) rectification (reformation): - correction. (*Strong's*)

NOTE: After you have turned in tests (times up, put your pencils down) it is time for the teacher to grade them. There will be lots of circled errors in the proverbial red ink to show you not only where you missed things, but the areas not circled, will show where you got things right. I like the idea in the definition of "straightening up again."

Again, the Word is the standard by which we measure the correct answers.

TRAINING/INSTRUCTION: Paideia (pahee-di'-ah)=From G3811; tutorage, that is, education or training; by implication disciplinary correction: - chastening, chastisement, instruction, nurture. G3811: paideuo (pahee-dyoo'-o)=From G3816; to train up a child, that is, educate, or (by implication) discipline (by punishment): - chasten (-ise), instruct, learn, teach. G3816: pais (paheece)=a boy (as often beaten with impunity), or (by analogy) a girl, and (generally) a child; specifically a slave or servant (especially a minister to a king; and by eminence to God): - child, maid (-en), (man) servant, son, young man. (*Strong's*)

NOTE: Once you have been taught the facts, been tested in what you have been taught, and then graded and shown the correct information where you made mistakes, you are now ready for instruction. I received my Black Belt, after years of training and a grueling testing time. As the coveted belt was tied around my waist, I was informed, "Now you are ready to learn." We began to be trained in what we had learned. When I received my Masters in Speech, and I set out in the real world to start my job in what I had spent years learning, we had to do a one year paid position called a C.F.Y. (Clinical Fellowship Year), where we worked under a supervisor to put into practice what we had learned in school. So it is with the tutelage of the Word. We are now ready to continue to be trained or instructed by practical example. The apostle Paul mentioned this in his letter to the church at Philippi.

> *"The things you have learned and received and heard and seen in me, practice these things; and the God of peace shall be without you."*

Philippians 4:9

The end justifies the means to be adequate and equipped in righteousness for the purpose of good works. You cannot effectively do good works apart from the Word of God.

THE HIDDEN WORD

> *"How can a young man keep his way pure? By keeping it according to Thy Word."*

Psalm 119:9

> *"Thy Word have I hid in my heart that I might not sin against Thee."*

Psalm 119: 11

The longest chapter in the Bible, Psalm 119, focuses on the importance of the Word of God in the life of the believer. The issues of purity are directly linked to the relationship with the Word of God. The secret is out. Hide the Word of God in your heart, you will not sin against God, and your way will be pure, because you kept, treasured, pondered on the Word of God and actually did what it said to do.

CHAPTER EIGHT
THE LOGOS-RHEMA CONNECTION

As we have seen, there is the natural words and language that we use for communication, and there is the supernatural words and language that we use to communicate with God and utilize here on planet Earth as we walk by faith and not by sight.

In the English language, we tend to use one word for many meanings. For example, I love hot dogs, I love music, I love my wife, I love God; not necessarily in that order. Each word is an expression of love, but I can, without a doubt, guarantee you that my love for hot dogs and my love for Brenda, my wife of 42 plus years is not the same love. In the Greek language, they have multiple words for multiple expressions. Take the word, "love" for example. There are at least four words for "love."

Phileo: (phil-lay-oh) This is a brotherly love, love for mankind. It is where we get the name of a city, Philadelphia (the city of brotherly love).

Storge': (store-gay) This is familial type love, the love of a parent for a child. I think of a stork bringing the one that we storge'.

Eros: (eh-r-oh-s)This is a sensual love that is more than just sexual. It is a love that appeals to the senses, so I would put in my love for hot dogs in this category as well as my love for Brenda in the romantic vain.

Agape': (uh-gop-a) This is the love that we attribute to the God kind of love, that is a giving love with no strings attached.

Each of these loves is wonderful and needed, but if the first three are not ruled by agape' we have turned our love into lust. Even some who claims to have this type of agape' love towards others is sometimes a hit-or-miss and can be termed as, "sloppy agape."

The same thing occurs with the word, "word." In the Bible we have two words for "word," word that is distinct and intertwines. Those words are logos and rhema. We saw that in John 1:1 that Jesus is the Logos.

WORD: Logos (log'-os)=From G3004; something said (including the thought); by implication a topic (subject of discourse), also reasoning (the mental faculty) or motive; by extension a computation; specifically (with the article in John) the Divine Expression (that is, Christ): - account, cause, communication, X concerning, doctrine, fame, X have to do, intent, matter, mouth, preaching, question, reason, + reckon, remove, say (-ing), shew, X speaker, speech, talk, thing, + none of these things move me, tidings, treatise, utterance, word, work. G3004: lego

(leg'-o)=A primary verb; properly to "lay" forth, that is, (figuratively) relate (in words [usually of systematic or set discourse; whereas G2036 and G5346 generally refer to an individual expression or speech respectively; while G4483 is properly to break silence merely, and G2980 means an extended or random harangue]); by implication to mean: - ask, bid, boast, call, describe, give out, name, put forth, say (-ing, on), shew, speak, tell, utter. (*Strong's*)

RHEMA: rhe ma (hray'-mah)=From G4483; an utterance (individually, collectively or specifically); by implication a matter or topic (especially of narration, command or dispute); with a negative naught whatever: - + evil, + nothing, saying, word. G4483: rheo (hreh'-o)=For certain tenses of which a prolonged form (ε□ ρε□ ω ereo) is used; and both as alternate for G2036; perhaps akin (or identical) with G4482 (through the idea of pouring forth); to utter, that is, speak or say: - command, make, say, speak (of). (*Strong's*)

These two words are like the two sides of a coin. Both different views of the same concept of the word, "word." The idea of *logos* is like a logo of a company that is designed to reflect the product. *Rhema* is experiential in nature. *Logos* is a general word to everyone, while *rhema* is a more specific, personal word.

LOGOS

Here are a few examples of the Word (logos) from the Word of God. (The emphasis on the following scriptures is mine.)

"In the beginning was the Word [logos], and the Word [logos] was with God, and the Word [logos] was God."

John 1:1

"The seed is the word [logos] of God."

Luke 8:11

"Holding forth (fast) the word [logos] of life."

Philippians 2:16

"Study to show thyself approved unto God, a workman that needeth not to be ashamed, rightly dividing the word [logos] of truth."

II Timothy 2:15

"For the word [logos] of God is quick, and powerful."

Hebrews 4:12

"Being born again, not of corruptible seed, but of incorruptible, by the word [logos] of God, which liveth and abideth forever."

I Peter 1:23

This logos is for everyone and available for everyone and anyone (aka whosoever) that would believe it. People can experience this Word, but they have to choose to believe (trust in, cling to, rely on) it.

RHEMA

Here are some examples of the Word (rhema) from the Word of God. (The emphasis on the following scriptures is mine.)

"So then faith cometh by hearing, and hearing by the word [rhema] of God."

Romans 10:17

"And take the helmet of salvation, and the sword of the Spirit, which is the word [rhema] of God."

Ephesians 6:17

"Husbands, love your wives, even as Christ also loved the church, and gave himself for it; That he might sanctify and cleanse it with the washing of water by the word [rhema]."

Ephesians 5:25–26

"If ye abide in me, and my words [rhema] abide in you, ye shall ask what ye will, and it shall be done unto you."

John 15:7

When Jesus told Peter to cast the fishing nets on the other side of the boat, Peter answered, "Master, we have toiled all the night, and have taken nothing: nevertheless at thy word [rhema] I will let down the net."

Luke 5:4-5

When the angel told Mary that she would have a child, "Mary said, Behold the handmaid of the Lord; be it unto me according to thy word [rhema]."

Luke 1:38

Simeon recalled the promise that he would see Christ before he died: "Now lettest thou thy servant depart in peace, according to thy word [rhema]."

Luke 2:29

God gave John the message he was to preach as a forerunner to Christ: "The word [rhema] of God came unto John."

Luke 3:2

God reminded Peter of His Word: "Then remembered I the word [rhema] of the Lord, how that he said, John indeed baptized with water; but ye shall be baptized with the Holy Ghost."

Acts 11:16

Jesus told Peter he would deny Him.

"Peter remembered the word [rhema] of Jesus, which said unto him, Before the cock crow, thou shalt deny me thrice."

Matthew 26:75

This Word (rhema) is taking the universal Word, and

believing it and acting upon it. If the word is to come out on the water, we step out of the boat. If news comes of an immaculate conception, accept it.

NOTE: Both words, *logos* and *rhema*, are important and vital. One is not better than the other, but are used in conjunction with one another.

Many years ago, back in 1972, I worked for a sign company. At this company, we would make the signs for a particular company or product and then lighted and placed high in the sky. Someone would design the logo that would then be placed on a frame with lights, and then lifted up on businesses or signs in the air, so people could see it and know where they could purchase the product.

When the company Esso gas changed its logo to Exxon, I knew it before much of the populace. I remember going down the interstate once the new logo was revealed and telling Brenda that I knew that was going to happen. Of course, she oohed and aahed over my wonderfulness. When you are driving down the road at night, you may see the sign shining in the night, letting you know that if you need gas, you can get off the interstate, pull in and fill up; or you can ignore the sign and drive on by and eventually run out of gas. The logo reveals where you can experience getting gas.

To me, this exhibits the Logos-Rhema Connection. Jesus is the Logos, the reflection and radiance of God and, when He is lifted up, it is for whosoever can come and experience salvation, if you believe. If you don't believe, pull in and receive the gas, you will eventually run out of gas. So many times, we are running on the fumes of our own self-righteousness and eventually run out of gas.

"And I, if I be lifted up from the earth, will draw all men to Myself. But He was saying this to indicate the kind of death by which He was to die."

John 12:32-33

Jesus related to this lifting up with an example from the Old Testament. In Numbers 21: 1-8, it is recorded that—after the Lord had given them a victory against their enemies—the people of Israel grumbled and complained against Moses and about the Lord delivering them from Egypt to die in the wilderness, where there was no water and only loathsome food to eat. The Lord sent serpents that bit the people and they died. When the people came to Moses confessing their sins, they asked him to intercede for them, which he did. The answer from God was for Moses to make a bronze serpent, put it on a pole, lift it up; those who looked upon the lifted-up serpent would live.

"And Moses made a bronze serpent and set it on the standard (pole); and it shall come about that everyone who is bitten, when he looks at it, he shall live."

Numbers 21:9

The serpent would be the logos and the looking upon it is the rhema. This is reflective of what happened to Jesus that He Himself used.

"And as Moses lifted up the serpent in the wilderness, even so must the Son of Man be lifted up; that whoever believes may in Him have eternal life. For God so loved the world that He gave His only begotten Son, that whosoever believes in Him should not perish but have everlasting life."

John 3:14-16

Again, Jesus is the Logos, lifted up for all to see, but

unless you see and believe (trust in, cling to and rely on) in Him, you will not experience what is available and have the full tank of everlasting life.

The bottom line about the Logos-Rhema Word is that both are thoughts of God and both are expressions of His thought. Both are needed to function in this natural world. When He speaks universally to the world, all the whosoevers in the world have an opportunity to experience what He universally offers, by His logos Word, and experience and obey His specific rhema Word.

CHAPTER NINE
THE PROPRIOCEPTION PRESENCE

Proprioception (pro-pre-o-sep-shun) is the ability by which we are able to internally monitor our speech and sound output. This is done by auditory (sound) and tactile (touch) feedback. When there is a discrepancy in that feedback, we either self-adjust or adapt. Of course, that is when your friendly neighborhood Speech Pathologist is called in to evaluate and treat the problem. This thing called proprioception is broken down into two components: (1) kinesthesia (awareness of bodily movement and position (2) taction (sense of touch or contact).

NOTE: I dedicate this chapter to Wayne Berry (aka the Sonic Ninja) who will be the one who truly understands what I'm talking about.

Words are a combination of vowels and consonants. According to *Terminology of Communication Disorders Speech-Language-Hearing,* a vowel is "a voiced speech sound resulting from unrestricted passage of the air stream through the mouth or nasal cavity without audible friction or stoppage." A consonant is defined as, "conventional speech sound made, with (voiced) or without (voiceless) vocal fold vibration by certain successive contractions of the articulatory muscles which modify, interrupt, or obstruct the expired air stream so that its pressure is raised." The bottom line definition of both is that air flows, and the mouth places the tongue in certain positions to produce a combination of vowel/consonant (VC) sounds with resultant words. Without this physical and aural thing called proprioception, we would have no clue if our articulators and voicing are being properly formed for proper articulation of words. But when proprioception is functioning properly, we can monitor and express our thoughts fluently.

We have this same concept in our spiritual lives. There is something called the presence of the Lord, where we sense and move in concert with His Spirit and we can live out the expression of God within us outwardly. This is manifested in what we call *grace*.

GRACE: Charis (khar'-ece)=From G5463; graciousness (as gratifying), of manner or act (abstract or concrete; literal, figurative or spiritual; especially the divine influence upon the heart, and its reflection in the life; including gratitude): - acceptable, benefit, favour, gift, grace (-ious), joy liberality, pleasure, thank (-s, -worthy). G5463: chairo (khah'ee-ro)=A primary verb; to be full of "cheer", that is, calmly happy or well off; impersonal especially as a salutation (on meeting or parting), be well: - farewell, be glad, God speed, greeting, hail, joy (-fully), rejoice. (*Strong's*)

This thing called grace is an inside-out job. It is influence, and not only influence, but divine influence. The cause-and-effect of this divine influence is the reflection in the life. To me that is one aspect of proprioception where there is a heavenly kinesthesia (awareness of spiritual movement) and holy taction (a sense of touch or contact) within us and a reflection in our lives.

This leads us to the words *presence* and *glory*. Both of these words speak of a place to be and, when we are in this place, we are to perceive and move accordingly. There are other words in the Hebrew and Greek language but, for our purposes, we will only deal with a few of them. To be in His presence is to be in His glory. The old Charismatic movement saying was that we wanted to be "under the spout where His glory comes out." There is a song lyric that declares that when we come into the presence of the living Lord, we will be changed.

PRESENCE: pa ni☐ ym (paw-neem')=the face (as the part that turns); used in a great variety of applications (literally and figuratively. (*Strong's*)

PRESENCE: eno pion (en-o'-pee-on)= in the face of (literally or figuratively): - before, in the presence (sight) of, to. (*Strong's*)

This presence in both the Greek and Hebrew language has something in common: the face. To be in the presence of someone is to be in close enough proximity to see their face. The Hebrew definition adds the phrase, "as the part that turns." To me this speaks of the head (with the face) sitting on the neck which turns the head. I have used a phrase that I heard years ago, "I am the head of my house, but Brenda is the neck, and the neck turns the head anywhere she wants it to go." When we seek God, we seek His hand for provision, while we seek His face for approval. Unknown In karate, when we award a new belt after a student tests, Sensei Taylor will go to each child and shake their hand. As he shakes their hand, they will have their eyes looking down at the ground and Mr. Taylor tells them, "Hold your head up, and look me in the eyes when you shake my hand." Why would he want them to look him into the eyes? He explains to them, "When you look someone in the eyes, it shows them you have confidence."

When we come into God's presence, there are mixed emotions. There is a coming into the presence that evokes fear and trembling and also a coming into the presence of Someone who loves us and is known as "Abba Father" or the intimate word for our relationship, "Daddy." His desire for us is to come in with confidence.

> *"Since therefore brethren we have confidence to enter the holy place by the blood of Jesus, by a new and living way which He inaugurated for us through the veil, that is His flesh, and since we have a great priest over the house of God, let us draw near with a sincere heart full of assurance of faith, having our hearts sprinkled clean from an evil conscience and our bodies washed with pure water."*

Hebrews 10:19-22

God's desire is for us to be in His presence. This is how man was created. Remember, the word *presence* speaks of a face. When God formed man of dust from the ground, He breathed His breath into man's nostrils. Now I know that God could have blown His breath from Heaven, but it seems to me that it was a face-to-face action. Some Bible teachers have said this was the first time that CPR was administered—with the twist that this was not an act of resuscitation but the first breath taken—that was face-to-face, mouth-to-nostril. resulting in, "man became a

81

living being/soul." (Genesis 2:7)

When Adam and Eve chose to disobey God in the Garden, they realized they were naked and they were ashamed. They clumsily tried to cover up with fig leaves, and hid from His presence.

> *"And they heard the sound of the Lord God walking in the Garden in the cool of the day, and the man and his wife hid themselves from the presence (face) of the Lord God among the trees of the Garden."*
>
> Genesis 3:8

Back in 1967, when I was sixteen years old, I met Elvis Presley. It was on a Sunday afternoon, behind RCA Recording Studio (Studio B). There were about twenty people, all milling around talking, laughing, anticipating the appearance of Elvis. I had been listening to Elvis on records since 1957, at the tender age of six years old.

At one point, some guy came out and told us that the recording session had been canceled and we needed to go home. We knew that he was lying. Within five minutes, a large Cadillac rolled through the alley, the doors flew open and out came Elvis in all his glory, bigger than life. We were *in his presence*. It was a surreal experience. The man whom I had been listening to for the last ten years was now standing before me. I experienced multiple emotions being in the presence of the *king of rock and roll*; joy, happiness, awe, fear and emotional upheaval. After he signed autographs and went in to record, my friends and I got back in the car. I began to cry.

Someone asked, "Why are you crying?"

All I could say was, "I don't know." There was emotional

release for me because I had been in his presence.

The question is, "How much more will being in the presence, face-to-face with the King of Kings and the Lord of Lords affect me spirit, soul, and body?" Of course, as we come into His presence, we will most likely have our face down until He calls us up.

Moses spoke with God, in God's presence.

PRESENCE: pa n☐ym (paw-neem')=Plural (but always used as a singular) of an unused noun (פנה pa neh, paw-neh'; from 6437); the face (as the part that turns); used in a great variety of applications (literally and figuratively (*Strong's*)

> *"Thus the LORD used to speak to Moses face to face, just as a man speaks to his friend. When Moses returned to the camp, his servant Joshua, the son of Nun, a young man, would not depart from the tent."*
>
> Exodus 33:11

Moses had a commission from God to "bring up this people" (Exodus 33:12) Moses desired favor and direction from the Lord:

> *"...if I have found favor in Thy sight, let me know thy ways, that I may know Thee, so that I may find favor in Thy sight..."*
>
> Exodus 33:13

God responded to Moses request:

> *"...My presence shall go with you, and I will give you rest."*
>
> Exodus 33:14

When Moses requested to "see Thy glory," God told Him,

"...you cannot see My face, for no man can see Me and live!"

GLORY: ka bo d ka bo d (kaw-bode', kaw-bode')=From H3513; properly weight; but only figuratively in a good sense, splendor or copiousness: - glorious (-ly), glory, honour (-able). H3513: ka bad ka be d (kaw-bad, kaw-bade')=A primitive root; to be heavy, that is, in a bad sense (burdensome, severe, dull) or in a good sense (numerous, rich, honorable); causatively to make weighty (in the same two senses): - abounding with, more grievously afflict, boast, be chargeable, X be dim, glorify, be (make) glorious (things), glory, (very) great, be grievous, harden, be (make) heavy, be heavier, lay heavily, (bring to, come to, do, get, be had in) honour (self), (be) honourable (man), lade, X more be laid, make self many, nobles, prevail, promote (to honour), be rich, be (go) sore, stop. (*Strong's*)

NOTE: This restriction of seeing God's glory is not a punishment, but protection. Moses could interact as a friend face-to-face but, to experience the *full on* effect of God's glory (the heavy of the Lord) would kill Moses.

NOTE TO THE NOTE: I have been in the presence of the Lord and it is a wonderful experience. At those times as I was in His presence, I experienced the glory of God and it was overwhelming.

You might have heard of being "slain in the Spirit." This is where the weight of the Lord's *unrestrained glory* falls and...you fall out. If He did not restrain His glory, we would die. When we flippantly say, "Get under the spout where the glory comes out," we don't know what we are requesting. Moses didn't, but God made provision.

"Then Moses said, I pray Thee, show me Thy glory!"

Exodus 33:18

"And He said, I Myself will make all My goodness pass before you, and will proclaim the name of the Lord before you, and I will be gracious to whom I will be gracious, and will show compassion on whom I will show compassion. BUT He said, you cannot see My face, for no may can see Me and live!"

Exodus 33:19-20

NOTE: Moses has already been in God's presence and been face-to-face and did not die. Now God is saying you can't see My face because you will not live. I believe this speaks of two different places; *in His presence* and *the glory of God.* Much like a transformer that shifts down the flow of electrical current from the mighty turbines so that our houses can regulate the flow of power, so it is with God's presence and the regulate presence of His glory. God made provision for Moses as God passed by; "the cleft of the rock."

"Then the Lord said, Behold, there is a place by Me and you shall stand there on the rock; and it will come about, while My Glory is passing by, that I will put you in the cleft of the rock and cover you with my hand until I have passed by. Then I will take My hand and you shall see My back, but My face shall not be seen."

Exodus 33:21-23

Later, in the New Testament (the Skinny Part of the Book), this experience in the Old Testament (the Fat Part of the Book), this incident is referred to in conjunction with the transition from Old to New.

"Having therefore such a hope **(confident expectation of things to come)***, we have great boldness in our speech* **(yes, there that word is again)***, and are not as Moses, who used to put a veil over his face that the sons of Israel might not look intently at the end of what was fading away. But their minds were hardened; for until this very day at the reading of the old covenant the same veil remains unlifted, because it is removed in Christ. But to this day whenever Moses is read, a veil lies over their heart; but whenever a man turns to the Lord, the veil is taken away. Now the Lord is the Spirit; and where the Spirit of the Lord is, there is liberty. But we all, with unveiled face beholding as in a mirror the glory of the Lord, are being transformed into the same image from glory to glory, just as from the Lord, the Spirit."*

II Corinthians 3:12-18 (emphasis mine)

NOTE: We can be in His presence and we can see His glory because we are still hid in "the cleft of the rock." That Rock is Jesus.

For me, it's a two-sided-coin, with His presence on one side and His glory on the other side.

GLORY: ka bo d ka bo d (kaw-bode', kaw-bode')=From H3513; properly weight; but only figuratively in a good sense, splendor or copiousness: -glorious (-ly), glory, honour (-able). H3513: ka bad ka be d (kaw-bad, kaw-bade')=A primitive root; to be heavy, that is, in a bad sense (burdensome, severe, dull) or in a good sense (numerous, rich, honorable); causatively to make weighty (in the same two senses) (*Strong's*)

GLORY: Doxa (dox'-ah)=From the base of G1380; glory (as very apparent), in a wide application (literally or

86

figuratively, objectively or subjectively): - dignity, glory (-ious), honour, praise, worship. G1380: dokeo (dok-eh'-o)=A prolonged form of a primary verb δο☐κω doko (used only as an alternate in certain tenses; compare the base of G1166); of the same meaning; to think; by implication to seem (truthfully or uncertainly): - be accounted, (of own) please (-ure), be of reputation, seem (good), suppose, think, trow (*Strong's*)

Many people equate the presence and the glory of God with feelings, emotions, physical movement and goose bumps. As mentioned earlier, during the Charismatic—or Pentecostal movement—we would want to, "Get under the spout where the glory comes out." If we didn't experience some kind of emotional upheaval, then we must not have been in His presence. Now don't get me wrong. I enjoy the good times and feelings in a meeting; but sometimes you have to "walk by faith not by sight" or feelings. However, His glory, His splendor, his rich and honorable presence may have the Kabad Effect (K.E.), also known as "the heavy of the Lord." I have experienced this in my life as I am caught up in His presence in a service where we have been singing, praising and worshiping, and suddenly something shifts in the room; or at least it shifts in me.

My proprioception kicks in and the kinesthesia—my awareness of bodily movement and position of God, His Spirit, His presence—kicks in and there my taction with the tangible, palpable sense of touch or contact with His presence and glory is experienced. The cause-and-effect may be seen in laughing, crying, repentance, dancing, running around the room, jumping or just falling out and laying on the floor, soaking it in as God speaks to us.

NOTE: The key to this proprioception with its (1) kinesthesia (awareness of bodily movement and position (2) taction (sense of touch or contact) is to be able to *self-adjust or adapt* as His presence and/or glory shifts and moves.

Nicolas Herman (1614-1691) joined a monastery and took on the name of Brother Lawrence of the Resurrection. He spent his life in servitude working in the kitchen and, in later life, became the repairer of sandals. After he died, his writings and observations were placed in a book called *The Practice of the Presence of God*. In his writings, spoke of being in the presence of the Lord in the midst of the mundane.

"I cannot imagine how religious persons can live satisfied without the practice of the presence of GOD. For my part I keep myself retired with Him in the depth of centre of my soul as much as I can; and while I am so with Him I fear nothing; but the least turning from Him is insupportable." (Brother Lawrence, *The Practice of the Presence of God*)

"We ought not to be weary of doing little things for the love of God, who regards not the greatness of the work, but the love with which it is performed." (Brother Lawrence, *The Practice of the Presence of God*)

"There is not in the world a kind of life more sweet and delightful, than that of a continual conversation with God; those only can comprehend it who practice and experience it." (Brother Lawrence, *The Practice of the Presence of God*)

To be able to move in the mundane things of our lives, and to be able to walk in the awareness of spiritual bodily movement and position of God and feel in our spirit (human spirit) and the tangible, palpable sense of touch or contact with His presence and glory, is the essence of spiritual proprioception. This brings up the questions; how can we get into His presence, and what is the cause-and-effect of being in His presence?

One of my favorite verses about His presence is found in Acts 3:19.

> *"Repent therefore, and return, that your sins may be wiped away, in order that times of refreshing may come from the presence of the Lord."*

Acts 3:19

I love to break down Acts 3:19 with the Triple R factor and the cause-and-effect.

- Repent
- Return
- Sins wiped away
- Times of refreshing comes
- From the presence of the Lord

REPENT: metanoeo (met-an-o-eh'-o)= to think differently or afterwards, that is, reconsider (morally to feel compunction): - repent. (*Strong's*)

RETURN: epistrepho (ep-ee-stref'-o)= to revert (literally, figuratively or morally): - come (go) again, convert, (re-) turn (about, again). (*Strong's*)

REFRESHING: Anapsuxis (an-aps'-ook-sis)=From G404; properly a recovery of breath, that is, (figuratively) revival: - revival. G404: anapsucho (an-aps-oo'-kho)=; properly to cool off, that is, (figuratively) relieve: - refresh. (*Strong's*)

Back in 1969, there was what was known as a "super

89

group"—comprised of Ginger Baker, Eric Clapton and Stevie Winwood—called Blind Faith. One of the songs written by Eric Clapton was, *In The Presence of the Lord.*

I like the part of the song where, instead of "the presence of the Lord," Eric sings, "in the colour of the Lord." Number One; I love the English spelling of the word color (colour) and Number Two; colour speaks of the broad range of hues and shades of my Lord. In the British vernacular, God is brilliant.

To wrap up this chapter, in the physical, natural world, the concept of proprioception is needed to monitor our speech. In the spiritual world, the concept of proprioception is needed to monitor the presence of the Lord and to be able to move and breath and be in His presence, so that when He looks at us in our face, and we look at Him in His face, we will see His approval or disapproval and our actions will be in accordance with His will.

CHAPTER TEN
COGNITIVE-LINGUISTIC REORGANIZATION

"For My thoughts are not your thoughts, neither are your ways My ways, declares the Lord. For as the heavens are higher than the earth, so are My ways higher than your ways, and My thoughts than your thoughts."

Isaiah 55:8-9

The scope of practice for a Speech-Language Pathologist is broad. You can specialize in a specific area or you can spread out in multiple levels of expertise. In reality, if you are out in the field (school, hospitals, nursing homes, home health) you will find that you will need a bag of tricks to cover a little bit of everything. I have found that in 21+ years of practice within the medical field, you never know what type of patient you will be treating and you will be expected to have some level of expertise. One thing I learned in my education in preparation to being an expert in Speech Pathology is to be able to research anything that may come up that you are unfamiliar with.

One area I have enjoyed learning about—in school and in the field—is *cognition*. The brain is a mystery and every day I find that I am the Sherlock Holmes of Speech

Pathology. That is the part of the job I love; being able to evaluate and pinpoint the area that needs to be worked on to help restore functional communication. As with many things, there is an intertwining connectivity with speech and thinking. This is called cognitive-linguistic skills.

According to *Terminology of Communication Disorders Speech-Language-Hearing* cognition is:

(1) General concept embracing all of the various modes of knowing: perceiving, remembering, imagining, conceiving, judging, reasoning.

(2) Act of process of knowing.

Linguistics is:

(1) Of or pertaining to language including knowledge of rules of sound (phonological), sentence structure (syntax), word meaning (semantics), and experiential usage (pragmatics).

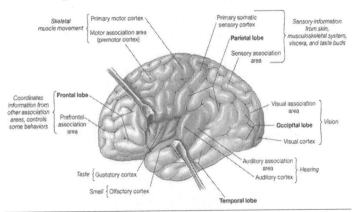

The combination of these concepts is called cognitive-linguistic skills, or the ability to know, perceive, remember, imagine, conceive, judge and reason in reference to speech, words and language.

The disruption of these areas affects our effectual communication and interpersonal skills. These difficulties can be brought about by multiple causes including a traumatic brain injury (T.B.I.), a cerebrovascular accident (C.V.A.) or any number of neurological diseases including Parkinson's Disease, Alzheimer's Disease, Multiple Sclerosis, etc.

Again, we are fearfully and wonderfully made and our brain is interconnected with our entire body.

Depending on where the brain has been affected will determine what function of the cognitive-linguistic system will need to be reorganized. Back in the olden days of research, the thought was, when a brain cell is dead, it is dead and that area would be gone. But as research has continued, the thought now is that there could possibly be regeneration of brain cells or, at the very least, there could be a reorganization of brain patterns to compensate for the dead brain cells. Remember, this is not a textbook, so we will not go into everything you wanted to know about the nervous system, but suffice to say, we are fearfully and wonderfully made. (Psalm 139:14)

One thing, among many things that I have learned from my Chiropractor and friend, Dr. Peter Camilio of Revolution Chirorpratics (Maximized Living), is how the brain is the control center for the entire body. When we are faced with dis-ease, dys-function and dis-comfort which interrupts our ease, function and comfort, the problems can be traced to the brain or impingements (subluxation) on our nerves hindering the flow of healing to every part of our bodies. Of course, most humans stop at the brain as their source of power, but the "missing link" with humanity and our earthly beings is the Creator of the body; God. This is where the healing flows. According to Dr. Pete, and medical science in general, "You have one brain. You have one spinal cord. You have 31 pairs of nerves. You have 75,000,000,000,000 cells. How many cells are controlled by each nerve pair? 75,000,000,000,000 / 31, each nerve pair's responsible for controlling ~ 2,400,000,000,000 (2.4 trillion) Functions." (Dr. Peter Camilio)

As a Speech-Language Pathologist in the medical field, I let people know that my scope of practice is not medical in nature, but more behavioral. By repetition of correct behavior, there is a shift or change in the thought, speech, swallowing patterns. There may be a re-routing of neural pathways around dead areas to reconnect and energize physical acts.

RENEWAL (Spiritual Cognitive Reorganization) OF THE MIND

While in the physical world we use various techniques to change thought patterns for cognitive reorganization, the cognitive reorganization process for our spiritual world is called 'renewing the mind.'

> *"Do not be conformed to this world--this age, fashioned after and adapted to its external, superficial customs. But be transformed (changed) by the [entire] renewal of your mind— by its new ideals and its new attitude—so that you may prove [for yourselves] what is the good and acceptable and perfect will of God, even the thing which is good and acceptable and perfect [in His sight for you]."*
>
> Romans 12:2
> The Amplified Bible

RENEW: anakaino sis (an-ak-ah'ee-no-sis)=From G341; renovation: - renewing. G341: anakainoo (an-ak-ahee-no'-o)=From G303 and a derivative of G2537; to renovate: - renew. (*Strong's*)

As we mentioned at the beginning of this book, we are hu-man beings made up of three parts—(1) spirit (2) soul (3) body—walking around as one unit. (I Thessalonians 5:23) When we congregate and interact with other people it leaves the general impression with them that is generated and projected to them by our renewed or un-renewed minds that will either be positive or negative. We project our inner soul-self outwardly to people we meet. How we react or respond to situations, circumstances, trials, troubles and tribulations is directly linked to our soul (mind, will, emotions). In the Sunday school class that I teach (The Ruminators) we use an example, usually to someone new in class, called 'Coffee Cup Theology.' Coffee Cup Theology is:

(2) Go to someone in class and move their Bibles, pens, papers.

(3) Place their coffee cup in front of them.

(4) Gently shake the cup so the coffee begins to slosh around in the cup.

(5) Begin to shake the cup harder forcing the coffee to spill over outside the cup onto the table in front of the person.

(6) After the shock and laughter dies down ask the question, "Why did coffee come out of the cup?"

(7) The usual answer is, "Because you shook the cup."

(8) The response is, "No, the reason coffee came out

of the cup, is because that was what was in the cup. The shaking only revealed what was in the cup."

So it is when we are shaken by the events in our lives; what is in us is revealed via our words and our actions.

The shaking in our lives can also reveal our trust, faith, peace, life in our lives. It is all hinged on what is placed in our cup (our hearts).

Our minds have been programmed by our experiences (good, bad and ugly), and will go into default mode. The way that we can reprogram, reorganize and change the default mode is by renewing the mind. It is all about a mindset.

"For what the Law could not do, weak as it was through the flesh, God did: sending His own Son in the likeness of sinful flesh and as an offering for sin, He condemned sin in the flesh, in order that the requirement of the Law might be fulfilled in us, who do not walk according to the flesh, but according to the Spirit."

Romans 8:3-4

The flesh becomes our default mode for the way we think, the way we speak and the way we do things. When we walk in the flesh, in an un-renewed mind, we are walking with no restraints. In class we put it like this;

"Unrestrained thoughts (what we think), produces unrestrained words (what we say), resulting in unrestrained actions (what we do)."

"Restrained thoughts (what we think), produces restrained words (what we say), resulting in restrained actions (what we do)."

Either way—unrestrained or restrained—we will be thinking, speaking and doing things with the cause-and-effect taking place.

In the book of Pro-Verbs (the book of Positive-Action), it speaks of people without a vision (insight).

> *"Without a vision, the people perish, but happy is he who keeps the law."*

> Pro-Verbs 29:18
KJV

> *"Without a vision (revelation), the people are unrestrained, but happy is he who keeps the law."*

> Pro-Verbs 29:18

PERISH/UNRESTRAINED: pâra‘ (paw-rah')=A primitive root; to loosen; by implication to expose, dismiss; figuratively absolve, begin: - avenge, avoid, bare, go back, let, (make) naked, set at nought, perish, refuse, uncover. (*Strong's*)

> *"For those who are according to the flesh set their minds on the things of the flesh, but those who are according to the Spirit, the things of the Spirit."*

> Romans 8:5

The idea of setting your mind on the flesh or the Spirit is all about mindset. Our mindset will either be un-renewed or renewed. It is a choice, but the default mode will be un-renewed. There is cause-and-effect if we do not develop a Spirit mindset.

> *"For the mind set on the flesh is death, but the mind set on the Spirit is life and peace, because the mind set on the flesh is hostile toward God; for it does not subject itself to the law*

of God, for it is not even able to do so; and those who are in the flesh cannot please God."

Romans 8:6-8

A renewed mind is a mindset that is restrained that affects what we say and do. A renewed mindset walks in life and peace. A renewed mindset is a mind of faith that pleases God.

"The steadfast of mind Thou wilt keep in perfect peace, because he trusts in Thee."

Isaiah 26:3

We are called to walk renewed in the spirit of our mind versus walking in the futility of the mind.

"This I say therefore and affirm together with the Lord, that you walk no longer just as the Gentiles also walk, in the futility of their mind, being darkened in their understanding, excluded from the life of God, because of the ignorance that is in them, because of the hardness of their hearts; and they having become callous, have given themselves over to sensuality, for the practice of every kind of impurity with greediness."

Ephesians 4:17-19

This walking is a learned (experience) process. Again, we walked in our learned (experienced) process that has been shaped by the good, the bad and the ugly things in our lives. We walk in the default mode of the flesh. But when we are in Christ (followers of Jesus), we learn a new walk by a renewed mind. This learning process is a spiritual process of changing the way we think and lining up with God thoughts.

"But you did not learn Christ in this way, if indeed you have heard Him and have been taught in Him, just as truth is in

Jesus, that in reference to your former manner of life, you lay aside the old self, which is being corrupted in accordance with the lusts of deceit, and that you be renewed in the spirit of your mind, and put on the new self, which in the likeness of God has been created in righteousness and holiness of the truth."

Ephesians 4:20-24

We keep coming back to the fact that we are fearfully and wonderfully made, from the top of our heads to the soles of our feet and everywhere in between. The thinking process in the physical is only as good as our thinking process in the spiritual. The problem is when mankind knows the truth but chooses to ignore what they know and do what they think, even when it violates the principles of God. After a listing of various things that God's creation does in the name of "professing to be wise, they became fools," (Romans 1:22) Paul brings it back to their thinking process:

"And although they know the ordinance of God, that those who practice such things are worthy of death, they not only do the same, but also give hearty approval to those who practice them."

Romans 1:32

In the book of Pro-Verbs, in the midst of wise advice about being careful who you sit down with to eat and drink, the writer drops in a nugget of wisdom about the thought process.

"For as he thinketh in his heart, so is he: Eat and drink, saith he to thee; but his heart is not with thee."

Pro-Verbs 23:7

If your mind is not renewed, as you think so you will

become, and how you think is how other people will see you and then you will begin to act in an un-renewed way. This is seen in Israel in the face of a promised blessing.

THE GRASSHOPPER SYNDROME (Numbers 13:1-33)

The Lord promised land to Abraham, and this promise extended not only to Abraham but to Isaac, Jacob (Israel) and beyond. Moses had set the children free from bondage in Egypt with the purpose of entering this Promised Land on an eleven-day journey, but it turned into a 40y-ear journey because of an un-renewed mind set.

"It is eleven days' journey from Horeb by the way of Mount Seir to Kadesh-barena."

Deuteronomy 1:2

"The Lord our God spoke to us at Horeb saying, 'You have stayed long enough at this mountain. Turn and set your journey, and go to the hill country of the Amorites and to all their neighbors in the Arabah, in the hill country and in the lowland and in the Negev and by the seacoast, the land of the Canaanites, and Lebanon, as far as the great river, the river Euphrates. See, I have placed the land before you; go in and possess the land which the Lord swore to give your fathers, to Abraham, Isaac and to Jacob, to them and their descendants after them."

Deuteronomy 1:6-8

In the book of Joshua, after Moses had died, they were prepared after 40 years of wandering and many people dying in the wilderness because of disobedience, to cross over into the land to possess the land. They were told to, "Be strong and courageous" (very courageous) multiple times in their crossing because they would have every opportunity to be weak and discouraged. Why? Because, in the Promised Land, there would be opposition by the people of the land.

In the thirteenth chapter of Numbers, we see the Lord instructing to Moses:

> *Send out for yourself men so that they may spy out the land of Caanan, which He was going to give to the sons of Israel.*
>
> Numbers 13:1

Moses was to send a man from each of their father's tribes and make sure each was a leader among them.

Moses sent them (for full listing see Numbers 1: 4-16)

Moses called Hoshea (Joshua).

JOKE ALERT: I would be remiss if I did not point out that Joshua was an orphan with no parents. That is why they called him Joshua, son of Nun (none).

When Moses sent out the elite force of spies, he gave specific instructions for their reconnaissance mission.

- Spy out the land of Canaan.
- Go up there up into the hill country.
- See what the land is like.
- See whether the people who live in it are strong or weak.
- See if whether they are few or many.
- See *how is* the land in which they live.
- See if the land is good or bad.
- See how the cities are in which they live.

- See if the cities are open camps or with fortifications.
- Is the land fat or lean?
- See if there are trees in it or not.
- Make an effort to get some of the fruit of the land because no the time was the time of the first ripe grapes.

These were their marching orders. Now remember, this is the land that God was giving them. It was not an effort to see if they could do it or not, but a matter of seeing that what God had said was true and that this was their land to possess.

"So they went up and spied out the land from the wilderness of Zin as far as Rehob, at Lebo-hamath. When they had gone up into the Negev, they came to the Hebron where Ahiman, Sheshai and Talmai, the decendants of Anak were. (Now Hebron was built seven years before Zoan in Egypt. Then they came to the valley of Eshcol and from there cut down a branch with a single cluster of grapes; and they carried it on a pole between two men with some of the pomegranates and the figs. That place is called the valley of Eschol, because of the cluster which the sons of Israel cut down from there."

Numbers 13:21-24

They returned to Moses, with mission accomplished. Now they were ready to report back to Moses and the people. They reported to Moses and Aaron, and the congregation and showed them the fruit of the land.

"...and they brought back word to them..."

Numbers 13:26

Remember that words and thoughts are powerful and can set the mood for victory or defeat. Here is the report from the brave, courageous spies:

- We went in to the land where you sent us.

- It certainly does flow with milk and honey and this is its fruit.

Here is where the report turns bad, preface with the word, *"nevertheless."*

Nevertheless:
- The people who live in the land are strong.
- The cities are fortified.
- The cities are very large.

Now, the second word that continues with the negative report is *"moreover."*

Moreover:
- We saw the descendants of Anak there.
- Amalek is living the land of the Negev.
- The Hittites, Jebusites and the Amorites are living in the hill country
- The Canaanites are living by the sea and by the side of the Jordan.

This is not necessarily the bad report. They were commissioned to find out these facts. At this point, Caleb (Joshua's right hand man) had to quiet the people. Apparently the report cause some grumbling and complaining.

> *"Then Caleb quieted the people before Moses and said, 'We should by all means go up and take possession (of the Promised Land), for we shall surely overcome it.'"*

> Numbers 13:30

Now, this is where the bad report was solidified. Twelve men saw the same things, but ten gave out a bad report and two gave out a good report.

> *"But the men who had gone up with him said, 'We are not able to go up against the people, for they are too strong for us'. So they gave out to the sons of Israel a bad report of the land which they had spied out saying, 'The land through which we have gone, in spying it out, is a land that devours its inhabitants; and all the people whom we saw in it are men of great size.'"*
>
> Numbers 13:31-32

Remember that we are talking about cognitive-linguistic reorganization from the physical speech perspective. We have talked about how what we think and what we speak determines what we do. In this Numbers passage we see that they saw, they processed the information in their minds and they spoke out from an un-renewed mind versus the renewed mind of Caleb. Caleb said, *"We should by all means go up and take possession of it, for we shall surely overcome it,"* (Numbers 13:30) while the other ten spoke from an un-renewed mindset said, *"We are not able to go up against the people, for they are too strong for us."* (Numbers 13:31)

THE ROOT OF A MINDSET

The key to the un-renewed mindset and the un-renewed speech and the un-renewed actions are found in Numbers 13:33.

- They saw the Nephilim (the sons of Anak).
- We became like grasshoppers in our own sight.
- So we were in their sight.

How they saw and thought about themselves in the reflection and shadow of the enemy was how they became in their own thinking (un-renewed) and was exactly how the enemy saw and thought about them.

Take your mind and wash it in the water of the Word and begin to reorganize your thought process and begin to speak and act as a man or woman of God and not as a defeated human, but more than a conqueror.

CHAPTER ELEVEN
FAILURE TO THRIVE (TASTE AND SEE)

"O taste and see that the Lord is good; How blessed is the man who takes refuge in Him!"

Psalm 34:8

When I started back to school—after my sojourn into the world of construction—I took a personal field trip with Dr. Kay Garrard, my Speech mentor, to the V.A. Hospital to meet with John Ashford, the director of Speech Pathology. Here is the word of wisdom he imparted to this student.

"Learn everything you can about swallowing. It is the future of Speech Therapy." (Dr. John Ashford CCC-SLP)

At the time there were no classes on swallowing and the dysfunction of swallowing, which is called dysphagia, other than a mention in some other classes. Today, there are entire classes devoted to swallowing and a plethora of seminars you can attend to add to your expertise in swallowing. I took his advice and, as a result, for every job I have had since 1993 until the present, I was asked what I knew about swallowing? On my very first job interview post-graduate school, the question was asked, "Can you do a video swallow?" My answer was a resounding, "Why yes I can," with the added caveat, "But I may need some training."

Now you may be asking yourself, "Self, what does swallowing have to do with speech?" Well, I'm glad you asked that question. The answer is that, for the most part, the same muscles and nerves that are involved in speech production are involved in the swallowing process.

Swallowing is an intricate process that we do reflexively thousands of times a day, but when there is a dysfunction of the swallowing process, this could be problematic to coughing, choking, dehydration and malnourishment, failure to thrive and even death. To understand dysfunction in swallowing, you must understand the proper swallowing function. Of course, by now you know that I will somehow be bringing the things of speech and swallowing in the natural back to the spiritual and see how we can become spiritually dehydrated and malnourished, even to the point of spiritual failure to thrive. But first let us take a look at the "normal swallow."

THE NORMAL SWALLOW

As we look at the normal swallowing process, remember that we are fearfully and wonderfully made.

Swallowing is sequenced, timed and controlled and anything that disrupts the sequencing, timing and control of the swallow is called dysphagia. In *Terminology of Communication Disorders Speech-Language-Hearing*, 'dysphagia' is defined as, "Difficulty in swallowing; may include inflammation, comprehension, paralysis, weakness or hyper-tonicity of the esophagus."

Within the Speech community there are disagreements on how to pronounce this word dysphagia. Some say "dis-FAY-jhuh" while others say "dis-F-AH-jhuh." To complicate matters more, there is a word for speechlessness called aphasia (uh-fay-jhuh) or dysphasia. For me, I am going with "dis-FAH-jhuh" for swallowing disorders and dis-FAY-juah for the language disorder, and to coin the song about word pronunciation of potato and tomato, "Let's call the whole thing off."

But back to the matter at hand; the normal swallow. We will look at the three areas individually, but we need to realize that they work as one unit to complete the swallowing function.

STAGES OF THE SWALLOW

There are four stages of the swallow.

Pre-oral stage: This is where, before food or drink are presented into the oral cavity (mouth), there is a physical reaction—based on what you see and smell—that sets into motion salivation and release of digestive enzymes used to help break down the food for processing in the body after you swallow.

Oral stage: This is where food/drink is presented into the oral cavity (mouth) and the food mixes with the saliva, is masticated (chewed) in a rotary fashion, formed into a bolus (a cohesive ball) and transferred from anterior (front) to posterior (back) of the mouth by the tongue to the place of the trigger to go to the next stage.

Pharyngeal (throat) Stage: This is where the bolus is transferred from mouth, throat, into the esophagus and into the stomach. Once this stage is triggered, multiple things take place.

- The epiglottis (leaf like structure) behind the tongue begins to invert (go down) so material will not collect between the tongue and the epiglottis (called the valleculae or valley).

- The vocal folds begin to close for airway protection.

- The larynx (voice box) begins to elevate and move forward (this is what you see when you swallow and your "Adam's apple" (aka goozle) goes up and down.

- The vocal folds are closed tightly, the epiglottis covers the larynx, the pharyngeal muscles squeezes the bolus towards the esophagus, as the food passes through two channels called the pyriform sinuses (on each side of the throat), through a muscle called the cricopharyngeal muscle (aka cricopharyngeous,) into the esophagus.

Esophageal Stage

The esophagus then squeezes the bolus down in two sweeping motions: the primary peristalsis and then a secondary wave cleaning up any remaining food.

The food arrives into the stomach to be processed to the body.

Did I tell you that we are fearfully and wonderfully made? (Psalm 139:14)

TIMING

The oral stage can vary from person to person. This

depends on your dental condition and your mental condition. But once the food has been chewed and transferred from the anterior to the posterior of the mouth, and it reaches the triggering area (the bilateral anterior faucial pillars), the time that it takes to go from the mouth to the esophagus is around 1-3 seconds. Anything longer gives more opportunity to go into the lungs (aspiration).

CONTROL

When what you swallow goes "out of control" and it controls you, then you have a problem.

EVALUATION OF THE SWALLOWING FUNCTION

As a Speech-Language Pathologist, I am called to do a swallowing evaluation to determine if the patient is able to swallow and, if they are swallowing, is it safe for them to swallow. Some of the problems associated with the swallow ranges from pneumonia to death.

We start off with an initial evaluation called the Clinical Swallowing Study, or the Bedside Swallowing Study. With this study, you can determine if there is a potential problem with the swallow or if there is a need for further in-depth evaluation.

One in-depth evaluation can be what is known as FEES (Fiber Endoscopic Evaluation of Swallowing), where the swallow is viewed via an endoscopic camera placed through the nose to view the swallowing mechanism.

Another in-depth evaluation is a VFSS (Video Fluroscopic Swallowing Study) where barium-mixed food and drink is presented via the oral cavity and you view the transit path of the food from mouth to stomach in real time.

These studies can determine where the swallowing function is breaking down, after which an individual treatment plan can be designed for the patient.

In your spiritual life, it is also a good thing to have an evaluation or test to determine your relationship with the Lord. Sometimes we go on automatic pilot in our faith walk and we become desensitized to our flesh or the sin in our lives.

> *"Test yourselves to see if you are in the faith; examine yourselves! Or do you not recognize this about yourselves, that Jesus Christ is in you—unless indeed you faith the test?"*
>
> II Corinthians 13:5

TEST/EXAMINE: peirazo (pi-rad'-zo)=From G3984; to test (objectively), that is, endeavor, scrutinize, entice, discipline: - assay, examine, go about, prove, tempt (-er), try. G3984: peira (pi'-rah=From the base of G4008 (through the idea of piercing); a test, that is, attempt, experience: - assaying, trial. G4008: peran (per'-an)=Apparently the accusative case of an obsolete derivation of πει□ ϱω peiro (to "peirce"); through (as adverb or preposition), that is, across: - beyond, farther (other) side, over. (*Strong's*)

If we don't test ourselves, before we realize it, we can enter into failure to thrive. In the physical, failure to thrive occurs when we begin to not eat or drink for various reasons. It could be related to emotions and anxiety, or it could be related to some swallowing difficulty that makes it hard for us to eat, resulting in eating and drinking less and using excuses like "I'm not hungry." What we are really saying it, "It is too hard to eat and swallow, so I just won't eat." We slowly become dehydrated and malnourished and lose the desire to eat and drink, and begin to fail to thrive which could lead to death. One of the saddest things I have seen over and over again in the areas of swallowing is when there is an abundance of food and/or drink in the presence of a person, but they will not eat or drink.

What is sad in the Kingdom of God is where there is an abundance of The Word of God (bread/manna/food) and an abundance of The Holy Spirit (Living Waters/well, rivers) and we will not eat or drink. Oh we may have been hungry and thirsty, but we quit reading the Word, we kept The Holy Spirit at bay and chose not to be obedient to the Spirit and Word, and slowly enter into the condition of failure to thrive.

In the physical, I have seen where we have determined there was a problem, resolved the problem and have seen the patient begin to thrive again. In the spiritual, we can thrive and revive as we begin to get some nourishment and hydration. In the physical it may take an adjustment in the diet texture, or beginning to eat multiple small meals, or have I.V. fluids placed, or a temporary N.G. Tube (nasal gastric tube) or a P.E.G. Tube (percutanious endoscopic gastric tube) placed in the stomach to have maximum nutrition and hydration presented. Once there is a return to ability to eat orally, these tube can be removed or can be left long term.

The goals I set for my swallowing patients are long term and short term goals. The long term goal is:

- "The patient will swallow in the safest, least restrictive manner for maximum nutrition and hydration."

The short term goals may include but not limited to:

- Change diet texture.

- Thicken liquids.

- Eat multiple, smaller meals.

- Utilize tactile (touch), thermal (cold or hot), gustatory (sour) stimulation.

- Various techniques to enhance swallowing function (supraglottic swallow, Musaka method, etc.

To get our spiritual deficient, failure to thrive patient back to maximum spiritual condition we recommend:

- Connect again with other believers.

- Read the Word.

- Ask the Holy Spirit to help you.

- Pray.

The will of God on Earth as it is in Heaven is not failure to thrive but success to thrive. Jesus came to give us life and that more abundantly. An abundant life to where we are not being overcame but we are the overcomers. Not to be defeated, and not just to conquerors, but to be more than conquerors. (Joshua 1:8, John 10:10, I John 5:4; Romans 8:31-39)

CHAPTER TWELVE
THE TONGUE (357 CALIBER)

"So also the tongue is a small part of the body, and yet it boasts of great things. Behold, how great a forest is set aflame by such a small fire."

James 3:5

According to the *Terminology of Communication Disorders Speech-Language-Hearing*, the tongue is defined as:

"(1) A highly mobile mass of muscular tissue covered with mucous membrane which is located on the floor of the mouth; it serves as an organ of taste and assists in mastication, swallowing, and articulation. (2) Primary organ of articulation, usually functioning in conjunction with the mandible to assist in the production of many different speech sounds; as a resonator, it modifies the shape of the oral cavity and alters the position of the soft palate, hyoid bone, mandible and pharynx."

In the chapter on The Proprioception Presence, we saw that the two components of proprioception, kinesthesia (awareness of bodily movement and position) and taction (sense of touch or contact), are needed for the tongue to be able to form sounds and manipulate food to set up for the swallow.

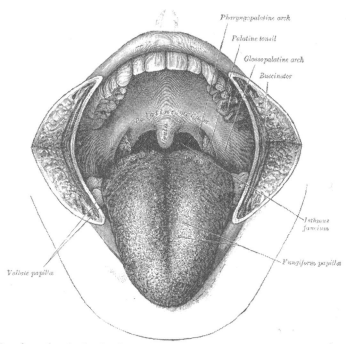

In the physical, dysfunction of the tongue can be caused by a stroke, a neurological condition, a malformation at birth or environmental in nature. You may have heard of someone being "tongue tied." This phrase is known as "ankyloglossia" which means that there is limited movement of the tongue. Usually it is because tongue is anchored by a short frenulum or frenum (the cord under the tongue that limits movement). Sometimes this is clipped but too often needlessly. Another aspect of the tongue is when someone has a stroke and they have slurred speech which is known as dysarthria. Also associated with a stroke is oral/verbal apraxia (in combination with language difficulty called 'aphasia'). Apraxia is a motor planning difficulty. The tongue may not have any muscular weakness, but they cannot figure out where to put the tongue.

So this thing called the glossal, the tongue, is an intricate, needed part of the body, and when it is out of control for whatever reason, it presents severe problems with our daily function. So it is with our tongues as related to our physical being. Remember, we are spirit (the core of who we are), soul (mind, free will and emotions), and body (flesh, blood, bones and most definitely the tongue).

NOTE: In a later chapter we will be looking at what is known as glossolalia (speaking in tongues). This is defined in *Terminology of Communication Disorders Speech-Language-Hearing* as "Unintelligible jargon which has meaning to the originator but has no meaning for the listener."

Remember our saying about being unrestrained?

"Unrestrained thoughts (what we think) produces unrestrained words (what we say) resulting in unrestrained actions (what we do)." (Unknown)

The tongue is the carrier of your thoughts by sound that is generated by airflow through the vibrating vocal folds, and words are formed by the articulators with the tongue being the primary articulator (in my mind). The mouth, the lips, the tongue are all involved in blessing or cursing. As our mouth goes, eventually so goes our actions. Now, let us see how this very small thing, the tongue, can largely affect our lives depending on how we control it.

In the Bible, the tongue is mentioned 129 times in 126

verses. We won't be looking at all of the verses, but you get the idea that the tongue is an intricate part of our spiritual lives.

TONGUE: glo ssa (gloce'-sah)=Of uncertain affinity; the tongue; by implication a language (specifically one naturally unacquired): - tongue. (*Strong's*)

The physical tongue is a revealer of the spiritual heart. It is also the means by which people of different cultures, countries and ethnicities communicate with one another.

In a previous chapter we talked about the people in the land of Shinar and the whole Earth using the same language and the same words. We saw that they communicated by speaking and the speaking was made possible, in part, by the tongue. As they communicated with each other with their own tongue (language,) using their physical tongue to form words, nothing was impossible if they purposed it. So God came down and scattered them so they could not communicate. (Genesis 11:1-9) They may have had their tongue (language) confused, but whatever language they now spoke, they still utilized the tongue in their mouths.

THE PROBLEMATIC TONGUE

What we speak can sometimes get us into trouble. Some have called this "foot and mouth disease" in comparison to "hoof and mouth disease" that various ruminants can get. "Foot and mouth disease" is where you open your mouth and stick your foot in it and say something stupid. Some have called this flow of stupidity from the mouth and tongue as "diarrhea of the mouth". It has also been described as "not getting your brain in gear before you speak." Another great description of the mouth is when we "shoot off our mouths." Our mouths are equated as a gun where we point our tongue towards someone and let loose with a barrage of word bullets with a drive by wording. If you shoot a bullet at someone, you cannot retrieve the bullet, it is going to hurt someone; the same thing with words that are shot out of your mouth. "Sticks and stones may break my bones, but words can never hurt me." Wrong! Words delivered with the mouth and tongue can go deep into a person and devastate them.

We all have different types and calibers of oral guns and bullets. Some have a 357 mouth, while others a snub nose 38, while others utilize a Gatlin Gun or AK47s, while others lob grenades and others just go all out with a nuclear, atomic bomb to devastate the human soul and spirit. Sometimes innocent victims get caught in the crossfire and we have collateral damage with our words.

TONGUES OF FIRE (The Negative Kind)

In the Second Chapter of Acts, where the Holy Spirit (the Promise of God) descended, there were tongues of fire present. These were the positive kind versus the negative kind.

> *"And there appeared to them tongues as of fire distributing themselves, and they rested on each one of them. And they were all filled with the Holy Spirit and began to speak with other tongues, as the Spirit gave utterance."*
>
> Acts 2:3-4

These were tongues of fire from God versus tongues of fire in our mouth. We will cover tongues of fire in a later chapter. For now let us look at the James passage about the tongue.

The tongue is linked to our entire being. The book of

James has much to say about this fiery part of the body. It is the reflector of our inward emotions. We first see the mention of the relationship of the mouth and the emotions in James 1:19

> *"This you know, my beloved brethren. But let one be (1) Quick to hear (2) Slow to speak (3) Slow to anger, for the anger of man does not achieve the righteousness of God."*
>
> James 1:19-20 (emphasis mine)

Verse 21 begins with "therefore" which refers back to what we just read that will relate to the coming verses. Our hearing and speech and controlled emotions will determine if we will have true religion or not. We see that we must be doers of the Word and not just hearers.

> *"If anyone thinks himself to be religious, and yet does not bridle his tongue but deceives his own heart, this man's religion is worthless."*
>
> James 1:26

> *"Pure and undefiled religion in the sight of our God and Father, (1) To visit orphans and widows in their distress (2) To keep oneself unstained by the world."*
>
> James 1:27 (emphasis mine)

Again, the link to this pure and undefiled religion is linked to the Word, to what we hear and what we speak and emotions under control.

As we continue this thread of thought in James, the tongue comes to the forefront with analogies of how a bridle and bits can control large animals.

> *"Now if we put the bits into the horses' mouths so that they may obey us, we direct their entire body as well."*
>
> James 3:3

119

So we see how a very small area can control a larger area in our lives. This is underscored with the analogy of a ship, a large vessel can be directed by a small rudder.

"Behold, the ships also, though they are so great and are driven by strong winds, are still directed by a very small rudder, wherever the inclination of the pilot desires."

James 3:4

The next verse begins with the two words, "So also" as we begin to compare the power of the little bitty tongue in the mouth to the bits and rudders.

"So also the tongue is a small part of the body, and yet it boasts of great things. Behold, how great a forest is set aflame by such a small fire."

James 3:5

Now we are getting to the crux of the matter about the power of the tongue. According to James 3:5-8 we see that the tongue:

- The tongue is a fire.
- The tongue is a small part of the body.
- The tongue though small boasts of great things.
- The tongue is the very world of iniquity.
- The tongue is set among our members (of the body).
- The tongue defiles the entire body.
- The tongue sets on fire the course of our life.
- The tongue is set on fire by hell (Gehenna).
- The tongue cannot be tamed by any one.
- The tongue is a restless evil.
- The tongue is full of deadly poison.

Wow, something so small—if not controlled like the bridle and bit in a horse's mouth or like the rudder of a ship—will cause big time trouble. This thing called the tongue/mouth was not designed to bring blessing and cursing. We cannot bless God and then turn around and curse the being who was created in His image. In the words of James, "My brethren, these things ought not to be this way." (James 3:9-10)

James continues with examples of how these things ought not be this way.

- A fountain cannot send out fresh water and bitter water.

- A fig tree cannot produce olives or a vine produce a fig.

- Salt water cannot produce fresh water.

Remember these examples are in reference to your tongue, which is mirror image of what is inside of you. You can't have it both ways.

Many years ago, I went with some other speech professionals to a class taught by a biochemist and nutritionist. He explained that, when we wake up in the morning with a coating on our tongues - it was the point of exit for poisons that were being released from our colon. He made the statement, "Our tongues are the mirror of our colon." Yuck!

When you think about it, in a natural way, the spiritual side is revealed. In this case, what is inside us of the flesh, will be manifested on our lips and tongue and our mouths as we either speak blessing or curse, positive or negative, God's Word or the d-evil's lies.

There are two sources: God or the d-evil.

"Who among you is wise and understanding? Let him sow by his good behavior his deeds in the gentleness of wisdom. But if you have bitter jealousy and selfish ambitions in our heart, do not be arrogant and so be against the truth. This wisdom is NOT that which comes down from above, but is earthly, natural, demonic. For where jealousy and selfish ambitions exist, there is disorder and every evil thing."

James 3:13-16

Our heart is revealed on our tongue and our actions if we don't restrain our words.

NOTE: Cussing is usually not socially acceptable in polite company. There are many intellectual people who cuss like sailors (including women), so you know that their use of foul language is not because they do not know other words to utilize. Usually, their cuss/curse words are based on angry emotion where they speak "unrestrained."

In contrast to the wisdom from above we see in James 3:17-18 that it is:

- Pure.
- Peaceable.
- Gentle.
- Reasonable.
- Full of mercy.
- Good fruits.
- Unwavering.
- Without hypocrisy.

The seed whose fruit is righteousness is sown to peace by those who make peace.

"Unrestrained thoughts (what we think) produces

unrestrained words (what we say with our tongues) resulting with unrestrained actions (what we do)." (Unknown)

THE GREAT TONGUE: CONFESSION

A confession has many different colors, positive or negative. We confess our sins, we confess the Word of God, we admit when we are wrong or a point of view is better by saying, "I must confess...," we confess a crime when we can no longer deny the evidence stacked up against us. But confession merely means saying the same thing that God says. If He says we are a sinner, we come into agreement with Him, if He says we are the righteousness of God in Christ, we come into agreement with Him. If He says that we are new creations in Christ and the old things have passed away, we come into agreement with that.

CONFESS: exomologeo (ex-om-ol-og-eh'-o)= to acknowledge or (by implication of assent) agree fully: - confess, profess, promise. (*Strong's*)

"For it is written, as I live, says the Lord, every knee shall bow to Me and every tongue shall confess (give praise) to God."

Romans 14:11; Isaiah 45:23

Because of Jesus' attitude, He was exalted. In Philippians 2:6-8 we see:

- He existed in the form of God but did not regard equality with God a thing to be grasped.
- He emptied Himself.
- He took the form of a bondservant.
- He took on the form of the likeness of men.

123

- He humbled Himself to the point of death on the cross.

"Therefore (because of what was presented in Philippians 2:6-8) God highly exalted Him, and bestowed on Him the name which is above every name, that at the name of Jesus every knee should bow, of those who are in heaven, and on earth, and under the earth, and that every tongue should confess that Jesus Christ is Lord, to the glory of God the Father."

Philippians 2:9-11

When our tongues confess that Jesus is Lord, we are yielding our will to Him, we are yielding our thoughts to Him, we are yielding our tongues to Him and coming into agreement with (aka confession) God about Jesus.

As we have seen, the confession of the tongue is the reflection of the heart. We see this in the language of righteousness. We see that, "righteousness based on faith speaks…" (Romans 10:6) Let's see what that righteousness is saying.

"But the righteousness based on faith speaks thus, Do not say in your heart, who will ascend into heaven? (that is to bring Christ down), or who will descend into the abyss? (that is, to bring Christ up from the dead."

Romans 10:6-7

We see what we should not say; so now let's see what we should say (confess with our mouth/tongue).

"But what does it say? The Word is near you, in your mouth and in your heart—that is, the Word of faith which we are preaching."

Romans 10:8

The two locations of this Word is (a) in your mouth (b) in your heart. The Word that is within and in your mouth must be released and this release is known as confession. Let us now look at how this released, confessed and believed Word is manifested.

> *"That if you confess with your mouth, Jesus as Lord, and believe in your heart that God raised Him from the dead, you shall be saved."*

Romans 10:9

Our very salvation is hinged on our tongue of confession. Let's see what happens when we take our tongue and believe and confess.

> *"For with the heart man believes, resulting in righteousness, and with the mouth he confesses, resulting in salvation."*

Romans 10:10

> *When you believe and confess, you will not be disappointed, "For the Scriptures says, Whoever believes in Him will not be disappointed."*

Romans 10:11

> *To activate this righteousness and salvation we must confess, believe and call upon Him. "For whoever will call upon the name of the Lord shall be saved."*

Romans 10:12-13

Not only is this thing called confession how we start this salvation and righteousness but, as we are on the journey and we sin, instead of denying that we have sinned, we are called to confess it.

"If we confess our sins, He is faithful and righteous (just) to forgive us our sins and to cleanse us from all unrighteousness."

I John 1:9

If we hold in our confession, we hinder God's ability to forgive and cleanse us.

WHO DO YOU SAY I AM?

Recently Brenda and I made a pilgrimage to Israel and toured the land of Jesus and the forefathers. One place we went was a place called Caesarea Philippi. It was at here that Peter (Cephas) made the confession that reverberates until this day. Here is the question/answer scenario found in Matthew 16:13-19)

> **Jesus**: *Who do people say that the Son of Man is?*
> **Them**: *Some say John the Baptist; some Elijah; and others, Jeremiah, or one of the prophets.*
> **Jesus**: *But who do you say that I am?*

NOTE: This is the question that each one of us must answer. Who do *you* say that Jesus is?

> **Simon Peter (Cephas):** *Thou art the Christ, the Son of the Living God.*
> **Jesus**: *Blessed are you Simon Barjona (son of Jonah) because flesh and blood did not reveal this to our, but My Father who is in heaven.*

NOTE: This was not an earthly revelation where you could go to the local school or library and study and come up with the answer. This was a spiritual revelation straight from Jesus' Father. Now with this revelation and confession (with the mouth/tongue), comes insight into the building of the Church and authority over the demonic activities of hell.

> *Jesus: But I also say to you are Peter (petros), and upon this rock (petra) I will build My church; and the gates of Hades shall not overpower it.*

PETER: Petros (pet'-ros)=Apparently a primary word; a (PIECE of) rock (larger than G3037); as a name, Petrus, an apostle: - Peter, rock. (*Strong's*)

ROCK: Petra (pet'-ra)=Feminine of the same as G4074; a (MASS of) rock (literally or figuratively): - rock. (*Strong's*)

NOTE: This is a contrast and comparison of Peter and the physical mass of rock that was surrounding them in this area. As we were standing at that location, you could look up to this surrounding mound of rock and imagine Jesus taking a pebble in His hands and saying, you are a piece of this larger massive rock. The Church was going to be built upon the massive rock of revelation that Jesus is the Christ (the Anointed One) and the Living Son of God, not on the pebble of Peter.

Jesus also spoke of the gates of Hades. As our tour group stood in this location, there was a cave in the side of this massive rock formation, where sacrifices (human) were made to the god Pan. Historically, this place is known as the Gates of Hades. Once again, we could visualized Jesus sweeping His hand over to this dark cave, and telling His disciples that when the Church is built on the rock of revelation that He is the Christ—the living Son of God— that no place of worship for anyone other than Himself would prevail against people who gather together as His Church.

CHURCH: ekkle   sia   (ek-klay-see'-ah)=From   a compound of G1537 and a derivative of G2564; a calling out, that is, (concretely) a popular meeting, especially a religious congregation (Jewish synagogue, or Christian community of members on earth or saints in heaven or both): - assembly, church. (*Strong's*)

Armed with this revelation that Jesus is the Christ, the living Son of God, the gates of hell/hades will not prevail against it. The spiritual warfare that will take place against the rock of the Church will not overpower it.

PREVAIL: katischuo   (kat-is-khoo'-o)=; to overpower: - prevail (against). (*Strong's*)

NOTE: If the spiritual forces are prevailing against the Church and you are a member of this Church, you might need to check out your mouth and tongue to determine exactly what you are confessing.

As a result of this revelatory confession that Jesus is the Christ, the Living Son of God, the keys of the Kingdom of Heaven were presented along with the power to utilize the Keys of the Kingdom.

> **Jesus:** *I will give you the keys of the kingdom of heaven; and whatever you shall bind on earth shall have been bound in heaven, and whatever you shall loose on earth shall have been loosed in heaven.*

BIND: deo   (deh'-o)=A primary verb; to bind (in various applications, literally or figuratively): - bind, be in bonds, knit, tie, wind. See also G1163, G1189. (*Strong's*)

LOOSE: luo   (loo'-o)=A primary verb; to "loosen" (literally or figuratively): - break (up), destroy, dissolve, (un-) loose, melt, put off. Compare G4486. (*Strong's*)

NOTE: This binding and loosing concerning spiritual things represents the authority that we have against the gates of hell trying to overpower the Church. Earth represents where we live in the physical; Heaven is where the authority flows from. There are two words for power: (1) exousia=delegated authority and (2) dunamis=dynamic ability. This dual power is how we are able to bind and loose in spiritual warfare. This authority and power is hinged on your confession with your mouth/tongue.

TONGUE CONNECTION

> *"Death and life are in the power of the tongue, and those who love it will eat its fruit."*
>
> Pro-Verbs 18:21

POWER: ya d (yawd)=A primitive word; a hand (the open one (indicating power, means, direction, etc.), in distinction from H3709, the closed one) (*Strong's*)

Another one of my favorite verses in Pro-Verbs deals with the mouth (where the tongue is located).

> *"If you have been foolish in exalting yourself or if you have plotted evil, put your hand on your mouth."*
>
> Pro-Verbs 30:32

So prideful plans can be thwarted by dealing where the come out. Put your hand on your mouth. This verse continues with what is taking place in the mouth and examples from the physical body.

> *"For the churning of milk produces butter and the pressing the nose brings forth blood; so the churning of anger produces strife."*
>
> Pro-Verbs 30:33

The milk would be our thoughts/words, our mouth/heart would be the churn and the speaking is the agitator and the butter is the cause and effect of the agitation/churning. Pressing the nose hard enough and long enough produces blood. If you churn, agitated words of anger in your heart/mouth it will produce strife. It is all about what you have in the churn/heart/mouth.

The positive side is replacing the words with uplifting words and love then you would have the paraphrased words from Elvis, "a hunka hunka of churning (burning) love."

Thank ya, thank ya very much. For those who don't know or care much about Elvis, thank you for enduring my moment.

TONGUE VERSES (English Standard Version)

Here are just a few of the verses out of the 129 verses that deal with the tongue for you to ruminate on.

> *"But no human being can tame the tongue. It is a restless evil, full of deadly poison."*
>
> James 3:8

> *"Death and life are in the power of the tongue, and those who love it will eat its fruits."*
>
> Proverbs 18:21

> *"Whoever keeps his mouth and his tongue keeps himself out of trouble."*
>
> Proverbs 21:23

> *"I tell you, on the day of judgment people will give account for every careless word they speak, for by your words you will be justified, and by your words you will be condemned."*
>
> Matthew 12:36-37

"There is one whose rash words are like sword thrusts, but the tongue of the wise brings healing."

Proverbs 12:18

"Let no corrupting talk come out of your mouths, but only such as is good for building up, as fits the occasion, that it may give grace to those who hear."

Ephesians 4:29

"If anyone thinks he is religious and does not bridle his tongue but deceives his heart, this person's religion is worthless."

James 1:26

"A gentle tongue is a tree of life, but perverseness in it breaks the spirit."

Proverbs 15:4

"To the choirmaster: to Jeduthun. A Psalm of David. I said, 'I will guard my ways, that I may not sin with my tongue; I will guard my mouth with a muzzle, so long as the wicked are in my presence.'"

Psalm 39:1

"There are six things that the Lord hates, seven that are an abomination to him: haughty eyes, a lying tongue, and hands that shed innocent blood, a heart that devises wicked plans, feet that make haste to run to evil, a false witness who breathes out lies, and one who sows discord among brothers."

Proverbs 6:16-19

"But I say to you that everyone who is angry with his brother will be liable to judgment; whoever insults his brother will be liable to the council; and whoever says, 'You fool!' will be liable to the hell of fire."

Matthew 5:22

"A false witness will not go unpunished, and he who breathes out lies will not escape."

Proverbs 19:5

"Not many of you should become teachers, my brothers, for you know that we who teach will be judged with greater strictness. For we all stumble in many ways. And if anyone does not stumble in what he says, he is a perfect man, able also to bridle his whole body. If we put bits into the mouths of horses so that they obey us, we guide their whole bodies as well. Look at the ships also: though they are so large and are driven by strong winds, they are guided by a very small rudder wherever the will of the pilot directs. So also the tongue is a small member, yet it boasts of great things. How great a forest is set ablaze by such a small fire!"

James 3:1-18

"So put away all malice and all deceit and hypocrisy and envy and all slander."

1 Peter 2:1

"For Whoever desires to love life and see good days, let him keep his tongue from evil and his lips from speaking deceit;'"

1 Peter 3:10

"A man who bears false witness against his neighbor is like a war club, or a sword, or a sharp arrow."

Proverbs 25:18

"For the word of God is living and active, sharper than any two-edged sword, piercing to the division of soul and of spirit, of joints and of marrow, and discerning the thoughts and intentions of the heart."

Hebrews 4:12

"But in the end she is bitter as wormwood, sharp as a two-edged sword."

Proverbs 5:4

"The good person out of the good treasure of his heart produces good, and the evil person out of his evil treasure produces evil, for out of the abundance of the heart his mouth speaks."

Luke 6:45

"All Scripture is breathed out by God and profitable for teaching, for reproof, for correction, and for training in righteousness,"

2 Timothy 3:16

"My son, be attentive to my wisdom; incline your ear to my understanding, that you may keep discretion, and your lips may guard knowledge. For the lips of a forbidden woman drip honey, and her speech is smoother than oil, but in the end she is bitter as wormwood, sharp as a two-edged sword. Her feet go down to death; her steps follow the path to Sheol;"

Proverbs 5:1-5

"If we confess our sins, he is faithful and just to forgive us our sins and to cleanse us from all unrighteousness."

1 John 1:9

"May the Lord cut off all flattering lips, the tongue that makes great boasts, those who say, 'With our tongue we will prevail, our lips are with us; who is master over us?'"

Psalm 12:3-4

"In the beginning was the Word, and the Word was with God, and the Word was God."

John 1:1

"With patience a ruler may be persuaded, and a soft tongue will break a bone."

Proverbs 25:15

"And every tongue confess that Jesus Christ is Lord, to the glory of God the Father."

Philippians 2:11

"From the same mouth come blessing and cursing. My brothers, these things ought not to be so."

James 3:10

CHAPTER THIRTEEN
TONGUES OF MEN AND OF ANGELS

"If I speak in the tongues of men and of angels, but do not have love, I have become a noisy gong or a clanging cymbal."

I Corinthians 13:1

WARNING: This chapter (and ensuing chapters) will be dealing with a very controversial subject. For centuries there has been strong disagreement about the validity of this thing called "speaking in tongues," miracles and healings, since any supernatural involvement with God has ceased.

On one side are those who believe that these things have ceased and that those who believe in such things are deceived and are intellectually deficient or Biblically illiterate. In the other corner, wearing the white trunks, are those who believe that there has not been a cessation of these things.

What is contained in this chapter is merely the opinion of this humble Speech and Language Pathologist. My colleagues may or may not agree with me at all. We study the development of this thing called language and come up with various theories of how it occurs along with the time lines of emergence and the standard of when there is a problem in the development of speech, language, articulation.

We may be able to evaluate, diagnose, develop a plan of care—and then treat these things in the natural—but when it comes to the supernatural, we are generally at a loss. I have found that as a behaviorist that I may be able to determine patterns that can be changed, but I can't totally understand the why of the matter.

As a believer in God, I can't prove Him (or His supernatural workings) in a test tube. Neither can I see the air that I breathe; but that does not stop me from taking in a breath. I have no clue of how computers work or how the internet functions, but here I am spending way too much time on it.

I like the song "Miracles" by Noel Paul Stookey, where he talks about how a scientist might be able to explain night turning into day, but he can't remove the wonder of a sunrise. He ends by stating that these 'miracles is a sign God uses to show the world the sacrificial love of Jesus.

I do not profess to have total understanding of this thing called "tongues of men and of angels." but I do have some personal experience with it. Since 1972, for me personally, it has changed my walk of faith.

This experience is linked with the Holy Spirit. Some would say that, when we received the Holy Spirit at the point of salvation, that was it. However, I have found that there was something more and that is what we will be covering in this chapter.

We will be looking at the baptism of the Holy Spirit, who is the baptizer; what happens when we are baptized; what is the difference of being baptized in water, the body of Christ and in the Holy Spirit. We will look at what took place at Pentecost and what took place beyond the Upper Room. We will examine how this relationship with the Holy Spirit, praying in tongues—both when we are with others and in private prayer life—affects our walk in Acts Chapter 29. Of course, there are only 28 chapters in the book of Acts, so Acts Chapter 29 is the acts of the Holy Spirit in our lives.

NOTE: The phrase "unknown tongue" is peppered throughout I Corinthians 12-14, but the word "unknown" is not in the original language. Paul is explaining that the hearer does not know what tongue is being spoken. If a Chinese man or woman came to me speaking Mandarin Chinese, that would be an unknown tongue to me. But the language is known to someone. So it is with tongues of men (known to certain people) and tongues of angels (known to the angels) and both known to God.

So here we go in a Speech Pathologist's perspective on tongues of men and of angels.

THE HOLY SPIRIT RECAP

In previous chapters, we have discussed the person of The Holy Spirit and His relationship with the Father and the Son and created man and wo-man. Here are a few bullet points:

- The Holy Spirit is at the creation (Genesis 1:1-3). He is hovering, sweeping over the face of the dark depths of water.

- The Holy Spirit is part of the Our and Us in the plan of creation of man/male/and wo-man/female. (Genesis 1:26-27)

- Throughout the Old Testament we see the Spirit of God on certain people (II Chronicles 15:1; 24:20)

- The first mention of the Holy Spirit being in someone. (Exodus 31:1-5; Exodus 28:3)

- This mention of the Holy Spirit being in a man by the name of Bezalel, the son of Uri, the son of Hur, of the tribe of Judah also points out the connection between the Holy Spirit in a human being and the effect on the natural. (Exodus 31:1-2)

- *"And I have filled him with the Spirit of God in wisdom, in understanding, in knowledge, and in all kinds of craftsmanship, to make artistic designs for work in gold, in silver, and in bronze, and in the cutting of stones for settings, and in the carving of wood, that he may work in all kinds of craftsmanship."*

Exodus 31:3-5

NOTE: The Gnostics believe that Spirit and human flesh cannot co-exist. That is why they say that Jesus could not be God in the flesh. But we see, and will see later, how the Holy Spirit of God is not limited by manmade concepts and reasoning. From the beginning until now, the Holy Spirit has been involved with the affairs of man and has not ceased.

Now the Holy Spirit is seen, as we have stated, throughout The Old Testament and, as we enter into the

New Testament, we see that the Holy Spirit continues to be involved with flesh and blood on planet Earth. In the Bible there are 415 mentions of the Spirit of God and 103 mentions of the Holy Spirit, for a grand total of 518 mentions of the person of the Holy Spirit, moving among humans.

THE HOLY SPIRIT AND THE BIRTH OF JESUS

We see angels and the Holy Spirit involved in the prenatal time in Mary's and Joseph's lives.

- Mary was found to be with child by the Holy Spirit (Matthew 1:18) Mary was getting married to Joseph but, before they had a chance to tie the knot, she was pregnant.

- Joseph was trying to figure out how to divorce Mary without disgracing her. There was an angelic visit in a dream letting him know that this child was the conception of the Holy Spirit. (Matthew 1:19-20)

- Elizabeth and Zacharias give birth to a son (John) who would be filled with the Holy Spirit while still in his mother's womb. (Luke 1:5-25)

- The angel Gabriel gives Mary the news that she—as a virgin—would give birth to the Son of God as the Holy Spirit comes upon her and she is overshadowed by the Holy One. (Luke 1:26-35)

- Mary visited Elizabeth and, when Elizabeth heard Mary, her baby leapt in her womb and Elizabeth was filled with The Holy Spirit. (Luke 1:39-45)

- When Elizabeth gave birth to John, Zacharias who

was unable to speak due to his unbelief about the conception of his and Elizabeth's baby, confirmed their son was to be named John and not Zacharias. Zacharias sang a song after he was filled with The Holy Spirit. (Luke 1:57-79)

- When the baby Jesus was brought to the temple to be circumcised on the eight day, there was a righteous and devout man name Simeon who was looking for the consolation of Israel (the Messiah). The Holy Spirit was upon him and revealed to him that he would not see death until he had seen the Lord's Christ (Messiah). Simeon came to the temple in the Spirit and saw and blessed Jesus as the One. (Luke 2:21-35)

- *"And the Child continued to grow and became strong, increasing in wisdom and the grace of God was upon Him."*

  - Luke 2:40

- The next time we hear of Jesus, He is 12 years old and amazing people in the temple, conversing with the teachers and elders; people were amazed at His answers. When His parents—who had been looking for Him—found Him, they question why He treated them this way. He responded that He was about His Father's business in His house. He subjected Himself to them and went with them; and Mary treasured these things in her heart. (Luke 2:4-51)

  "And Jesus kept increasing in wisdom and stature/age, and in favor with God and men."

  Luke 2:52

- The next time we see Jesus would be 18 years later, as He was about to encounter The Holy Spirit at the Jordan River.

THE ANOINTING OF JESUS AND HIS PURPOSE

"You know of Jesus of Nazareth, how God anointed Him with The Holy Spirit and with power, and how He went about doing good, and healing all who were oppressed by the d-evil for God was with Him."

Acts 10:38

"...The Son of God appeared for this purpose, that He might destroy the works of the d-evil."

I John 3:8

Jesus took the scroll of Isaiah and read from it to be more specific about this purpose. In Isaiah 61:1 and Luke 4:17-19 He reads:

- The Spirit (Holy) of the Lord is upon Me.
- He anointed Me to preach the Gospel (good news) to the poor.
- He has sent Me to proclaim release to the captives.
- He has sent Me for the recovery of sight to the blind.
- He has sent Me to set free those who are downtrodden.
- He has sent Me to proclaim the favorable year of the Lord.

After reading this passage, He closed the scroll, gave it back to the attendant and sat down. As the eyes of everyone in the synagogue were fixed on Him He said, "Today this Scripture has been fulfilled in your hearing."

(Luke 4:20) Jesus went about for three years doing this. He manifested "Thy Kingdom come, Thy will be done on earth as it is in heaven." (Matthew 6:10)

After 18 years of silence from the Scriptures about Jesus, He appears at the Jordan River, where his cousin John was dipping (baptizing) people in the Jordan River as they repented, in preparation for the coming Kingdom. The Pharisees and the Sadducees (religious leaders) were coming out wanting to be baptized, but John told them that he needed to see fruit (outward evidence) of their repentance. John then differentiated his baptism and the baptism of Jesus (who at that time was unknown to John as the One). (Matthew 3:1-10)

> *"As for me, I baptized you in/with/by water for repentance, but He who is coming after me is mightier than I, and I am not even fit to remove His sandals; He Himself will baptize you with The Holy Spirit and fire."*

Matthew 3:11

> *"And he was preaching and saying, After Me comes One who is mightier than I, and I am not even fit to stoop down and untie the thongs of His sandals. I baptized you with/in/by water, but He will baptize you with the Holy Spirit."*

Mark 1:7-8

> *"John answered and said to them all, As for me, I baptize you with water; but He who is mightier than I is coming, and I am not fit to untie the thong of His sandals, He Himself will baptize you in/with/by The Holy Spirit and fire."*

Luke 3:16

> *"John answered them saying, I baptize in/by/with water, but among you stands One whom you do not know."*

John 1:26

"And I did not recognize Him, but He who sent me to baptize in water said to me, He upon whom you see the Spirit descending and remaining upon Him, this is the one who baptizes in/with/by The Holy Spirit."

John 1:33

"For John baptized with water, but you shall be baptized with the Holy Spirit not many days from now."

Acts 1:5

So across the board in the Gospels of Matthew, Mark, Luke and John, we see that the baptizer in/with/by the Holy Spirit is, without a doubt, Jesus.

At this point it might be a good idea to talk about this thing called baptism.

THE DOCTRINE OF BAPTISM(S)

Many people get upset when you talk about more than one type of baptism. The verse they point to is Ephesians 4:4-6.

"There is one hope and one Spirit, just as also you were called in one hope of your calling, one Lord, one faith, one baptism, one God and Father of all who is over all and through all and in all."

Ephesians 4:4-6

Just to break it down in and easy to see format, let's put all the "ones" in bullet points. There is one:

- Hope
- Spirit
- Hope of your calling
- Lord
- Faith

143

- Baptism
- God
- Father of all

When the writer of Hebrews is laying out the basic/elementary principles about the Christ (Hebrews 6:1-2, we see:

- Repentance from dead works.
- Faith towards God.
- Doctrine/Instructions about baptisms/washings (plural).
- Laying on of hands.
- Resurrection of the dead.
- Eternal judgment.

When you see them laid out, they look progressive; as we repent and trust God, get baptized, have hands laid on and be raised from the dead and enter into judgment. But for our purposes now, let us look at the doctrine of baptisms (plural).

BAPTISM DEFINED

Baptisma (bap'-tis-mah)=From G907; baptism (technically or figuratively): - baptism. G907: baptizo (bap-tid'-zo)=From a derivative of G911; to make whelmed (that is, fully wet); used only (in the New Testament) of ceremonial ablution, especially (technically) of the ordinance of Christian baptism: - baptist, baptize, wash. G911: bapto (bap'-to)=A primary verb; to whelm, that is, cover wholly with a fluid; in the New Testament only in a qualified or specific sense, that is, (literally) to moisten (a part of one's person), or (by implication) to stain (as with dye): - dip. (*Strong's*)

In the Greek language, the word "baptize" or "baptism" is not translated from meaning to word; but is what is known as a transliteration from one type of letter to a corresponding letter.

TRANSLITERATION: verb (used with object), (trans·lit·er·at·ed, trans·lit·er·at·ing) =to change (letters, words, etc.) into corresponding characters of another alphabet or language: to transliterate the Greek /x/ as /ch/ for Christ. (*Dictonary.com*)

Β α π τ ζω (Greek)

B a p ti zo' (Transliteration)

Baptize (English)

Some say there was political and religious justification for transliterating verse translation so the meaning would be obscured. But, the bottom line is that "baptize" means to be wholly dipped into fluid and drawn back out again.

There are multiple types of baptisms. What differentiates one from the other can be broken down into three components.

- There must be a baptizer (dipper).

- There must be a candidate (one who is dipped).

- There must be an element (to be dipped in).

BAPTISM TYPES

BAPTIZER	CANDIDATE	ELEMENT	SCRIPTURE
GOD	FATHERS	MOSES/SEA	I Cor. 10:1-5
GOD	JESUS AND DISCIPLES	SUFFERING	Luke 12:50 Mark 10:38-39
JOHN	REPENTERS	JORDAN RIVER WATERS	Matthew 3:1-11 Mark 1:4 Luke 4:1-16 John 1:27
A MINISTER	REPENTERS	WATER	Matthew 28:19
THE HOLY SPIRIT	CHRISTIANS	BODY OF CHRIST	I Corinthians 12:13
JESUS	BELIEVERS	THE HOLY SPIRIT	Matthew 3:11 Mark 1:7-8 Luke 3:16 John 1:26 Acts 1:5

As you can see there are many baptisms and baptizers, but only one Spirit, one Body and one baptism into this Body. In the next chapter we will be looking at the Baptism in/of/with the Holy Spirit and the link with the tongues of men and of angels. (Don't you know that this Speech-

Language Pathologist gets excited about this stuff?) Let's continue to look at Jesus and the Holy Spirit, the One that Jesus will be dipping/baptizing us in/with/by.

INITIAL DOVE LANDING (Matthew 3:11-17; Mark 1:9-11; Luke 3:21-22; John 1:28-34)

After Jesus came and was baptized by John (to fulfill all righteousness) in the waters of the Jordan River, He came up out of the waters. Here is what happened next:

- The heavens were opened.
- The Spirit of God descended as a dove.
- The Spirit of God in the form of a dove lighted and remained upon Jesus.
- A voice spoke out of heaven, "This is My beloved Son, in whom I am well pleased."

This is the moment when Jesus was anointed with the Holy Spirit and with power. (Acts 10:38) Now Jesus would have a wilderness experience. In Chapter Six, "The Twisted Language" under the section entitled, "The Language of Lies," we discussed this temptation experience in depth. It is worth reviewing the relationship of that wilderness experience of temptation and the Holy Spirit that Jesus had just been anointed.

- Jesus was anointed with the Holy Spirit. (Matthew 3:16-17)
- Jesus was full of the Holy Spirit. (Luke 4:1)
- Jesus was led around the wilderness by the Holy Spirit. (Matthew 4:1; Luke 4:1)
- After the temptation was completed He returned to Galilee in the power of the Spirit. (Luke 4:14)

Remember, this is the same Holy Spirit that was at the point of creation and throughout the Bible, and is the One that Jesus will baptize us in and the One who will baptize us into the body of Christ. He is the same One who will distribute the gifts of the Spirit and the same One who has the fruit of the Spirit. He is the same Holy Spirit who gives us the ability to pray in the Spirit in tongues of men and of angels. No one will be able to say "Jesus is Lord" except by the Holy Spirit.

In closing this chapter, we will look at what took place as Jesus was anointed by the Holy Spirit and power.

ANOINTED FOR MINISTRY

> *"And Jesus was going about in all Galilee, teaching in their synagogues, and proclaiming the gospel (good news) of the kingdom, and healing every kind of disease and every kind of sickness among the people. And the news about Him went out into all Syria and they brought to Him all who were ill, taken with various diseases and pains, demoniacs, epileptics, paralytics; and He healed them."*

> Matthew 4:23-24

This was Jesus' Modus Operandi (M.O.) and it was all because He was anointed with (1) The Holy Spirit (2) Power (dunamis/dynamic ability). If you read the Gospels (Good News) of Matthew, Mark, Luke and John with this in mind, you will see Jesus healing/delivering in over 40 incidents over a three year period and everyone was the will of God on earth as it is in heaven.

BEYOND JESUS

This would have been a nice little story about a guy named Jesus who went around doing God things for three years and, when He died, everything came to a complete halt. Oh yes, there were a few more things done when His disciples received the Holy Spirit but, once the last apostle died, surely miracles, healings, tongues, etc. stopped. In John 14, we see Jesus prepping His followers that He was going to die, be raised from the dead, go away to prepare a place for them and then send down the Holy Spirit.

> *"And I will ask the Father, and He will give you another* **(allos/one of the same kind)** *Helper, that He may be with you forever* **(not for a short period of time)***."*
>
> John 14:16 (emphasis mine)

The word "allos" in contrast to "homo" means one of the same kind and not a different Helper. The Helper—that is one of the same kind as Jesus—is identified as The Holy Spirit in the next verse.

> *"That is the Spirit of truth, whom the world cannot receive, because it does not behold Him (a person not a force) or know Him, but you know Him because He abides with you and will be in you."*
>
> John 14:17

Jesus then again underscores who this Helper is.

> *"But the Helper, the Holy Spirit whom the Father will send in My name, He will teach you all things and bring to our remembrance all that I said to you."*
>
> John 14:26

This mention of the Holy Spirit coming is in reference to the passing on of the mission to continue after He has gone.

> *"Believe Me that I am in the Father, and the Father in Me, otherwise believe on account of the works themselves. Truly,*

truly, I say to you, he who believes in Me, the works that I do shall he do also; and greater works than these shall he do; because I go to the Father. If you ask Me anything in My name, I will do it."

John 14:11-14

WORKS: Ergon (*er'-gon*)=From ε ργω ergo (a primary but obsolete word; to *work*); *toil* (as an effort or occupation); by implication an *act:* - deed, doing, labour, work. (*Strong's*)

GREATER: meizon (*mide'-zone*)=*larger* (literally or figuratively, specifically in age): - elder, greater (-est), more. (*Strong's*)

The works were the healings, miracles, deliverances and oppressions removing.

At least at this point, His disciples would be taking up the charge and carrying on the works. Not only His works, but, according to Jesus, greater works, whatever that means. Jesus uses the word "because" to point to *why* and *how* they would be able to do the works; "because I go to the Father." What would happen when He went to the Father? The promise of the Holy Spirit would be sent back. Also, they would be able to ask anything in the authority of His name in reference to the works He will do it.

Some might think, *"That is fine and dandy but that was for His disciples, not us in this day and age."* Remember in John 14:16, the person of the Holy Spirit would be with them forever. We see that His disciples were commissioned by what we call The Great Commission to pass on, via teaching, whatever was passed on to them.

> *"And Jesus came up and spoke to them, saying, all authority (exousia/delegated authority/power) has been given to Me in heaven and on earth. Go therefore and make disciples of all the nations, baptizing them in the name of the Father and the Son and the Holy Spirit, teaching them to observe all that I commanded you; and lo, I am with you always, even to the end of the age."*

Matthew 28:18-20

"All that I commanded you" would include John 14:12-14. Again, as Jesus prayed to the Father in John 17 (the real Lord's Prayer) as He asked for His Father to "sanctify them by truth; Thy Word is truth," Jesus also underscored who He was praying for. It was not just those at that point in time that He considered disciples, but for you and me.

> *"I do not ask in behalf of these alone, but for those who believe in Me through their words."*

John 17:20

Their words are what would be spoken as they obeyed Matthew 28:20 and they taught them to observe all things that Jesus had commanded them, including doing His works and greater works. (John 14:12-13) Again, it is because of the connection of The Holy Spirit that was promised to be poured out.

CHAPTER FOURTEEN
THE ACTS OF THE HOLY SPIRIT

We continue our look at "The Tongues of Men and of Angels" by examining what is usually called, "The Acts of The Apostles." This book was written by Luke, who also authored one the Gospels. Both books are written to a man named Theophilus, whose name means "friend of God."

> *"Inasmuch as many have undertaken to compile an account of these things accomplished among us, just as those who from the beginning were eyewitnesses and servants of the Word have handed them down to us, it seemed fitting for me as well, having investigated everything carefully from the beginning, to write it out for you in consecutive order, most excellent Theophilus; so that you might know the exact truth about the things you have been taught."*
>
> Luke 1:1-4

> *"The first account I composed (see The Gospel According To Luke), Theophilus, about all that Jesus began to do and teach, until the day when He was taken up, after He had by The Holy Spirit given orders to the apostles whom He had chosen. To these He also presented Himself alive, after His*

suffering, by many convincing proofs, appearing to them over a period of forty days, and speaking of the things concerning the Kingdom of God. And gathering them together, He commanded them not to leave Jerusalem **(Luke 24:49),** *but to wait for what the Father had promised* **(The Holy Spirit)** *which, He said you heard of from Me, for John baptized with water* **(Jordan River),** *but you shall be baptized* **(immersed/dipped)** *with/in The Holy Spirit not many days from now."*

Acts 1:1-5 (emphasis mine)

"But you shall receive power when the Holy Spirit has come upon you; and you shall be My witnesses both in Jerusalem, and in all Judea and Samaria, and even to the remotest part of the earth."

Acts 1:8

These verses were to show the connection of the Holy Spirit to human beings in order to carry out the witness to the world. Yes, He uses human beings, but the bottom line is it's the acts of the Holy Spirit through the Apostles. They would not only physically verbalize what they had seen, but they would *be* witnesses. When the Holy Spirit comes into your life, you enter in to a new "state of *being*."

We have seen in previous chapters that Jesus was leaving planet Earth and when He arrived in Heaven He would ask the Father to send the Holy Spirit. (John 14:1-16; 26) After Jesus was crucified, buried in a borrowed tomb and three days later raised from the dead, He was seen by His followers and He gave them final instructions prior to His departure in the clouds; which is the same way that He will be returning. (Luke 24:49; Acts 1:1-11)

You may ask, "What does all of this Bible stuff have to do with a Speech Pathologist?"

Well, I'm glad you asked. The answer is, *everything*, especially in relation to this phenomenon of speaking in the tongues of men and of angels.

These followers of the Risen Savior returned to Jerusalem from their meeting with Jesus at the Mount of Olivet (olives) a Sabbath day's journey (a distance of 2,000 cubits, or less than half-a-mile) away. This was in obedience to Jesus's command in Luke 24:49; Acts 1:4.

> *"And when they had entered* **(the city of Jerusalem),** *they went up to the upper room…"*
>
> Acts 1:13 (emphasis mine)

NOTE: Brenda and I visited the location of the Upper Room where the disciples waited. It is a large room able to accommodate the one hundred and twenty mentioned in Acts 1:13-15.

During this time, they held a business meeting to choose a replacement for Judas, and they selected Matthias. (Acts 1:15-26)

THE SECOND CHAPTER OF ACTS

It was in the Upper Room that an event took place that changed the course of the world. The beginnings took place on the cross where Jesus was crucified in our place and became a curse so we would not be cursed. He was buried and then this cold, dead, propitiation (satisfactory substitute) rose from the dead on the third day. A few days later—after He ascended back to the Father—His followers (around 120 men and women) were gathered in this upper room in obedience to Jesus to wait for what was promised, The Holy Spirit, so that they would have the power to be His witnesses. When the day of the Feast of Pentecost—50 days after the celebration of the Passover—had come, something shook the place.

*"And when the day of Pentecost had come, they were all together in one accord **(place).**"*

Acts 2:1 (emphasis mine)

NOTE: The old joke (which I never get tired of hearing or telling) was that this was the first Honda Dealership, where they were all in one Accord. *Get it?* Okay…moving on.

Here is what took place:

- Suddenly, there came from Heaven a noise like a violent, rushing wind.
- The sound filled the whole house where they were sitting.
- There appeared to them tongues of fire distributing on the people.
- They (tongues of fire) rested on each of them (120 people men and women alike).
- They were all filled with the Holy Spirit.
- They all began to speak with other tongues, as the (Holy) Spirit was giving them utterance.

Something supernatural was taking place that was directly connected to Jesus going to the Father, and the Father sending the promise of The Holy Spirit, where God's *super* came on their *natural*. This was taking place in what would be known in the Greek as "ekklesia" (aka church).

CHURCH: ekkle sia (ek-klay-see'-ah)=a calling out, that

155

is, (concretely) a popular meeting, especially a religious congregation (Jewish synagogue, or Christian community of members on earth or saints in heaven or both): - assembly, church. (*Strong's*)

NOTE: Some claim it was this outpouring of the Holy Spirit that established the church. The outpouring of the Holy Spirit was poured out, the people received the dynamic ability (*dunamis*/power) to be witnesses. With this holy boldness to be a witness, Peter preached the word of faith of the Gospel about the death, burial and resurrection of Jesus. People believed and repented and were baptized and about three thousand souls were added. This was the establishment of the church. The Holy Spirit outpouring gave Jesus' followers the power to present to other people the opportunity to believe and become a part of the Church.

This God experience was not contained in a man-made building of stone, but spilled out into the streets.

> "*Now there were Jews living in Jerusalem, devout men, from every nation under heaven.*"

Acts 2:5

Remember, there was a celebration of the Passover going on; not only were those who were living in the city present at the time but there were thousands upon thousands of visitors to the city.

> "*When this sound (rushing mighty and speaking in tongues) occurred the multitude came together and were bewildered, because they were each one hearing them speak in his own language (dialect/tongue).*"

Acts 2:6

BEWILDERED : sugcheo (soong-kheh'-o)=Or συγχυ▢νω sugchuno soong-khoo'-no= (to pour) or its alternate; to commingle promiscuously, that is, (figuratively) to throw (an assembly) into disorder, to perplex (the mind): - confound, confuse, stir up, be in an uproar. (*Strong's*)

NOTE: One of the great debates about speaking in tongues is that "…God is not a God of confusion but of peace, as in all the churches of the saints." (I Corinthians 14:33) People use this verse to show that people who are speaking in tongues are not of God. If that were true, then those who were in the Upper Room who were filled with the Spirit—causing bewilderment, throwing into disorder, perplexing the mind, causing confusion and stirring things into an uproar—were not of God either. In the next chapter on I Corinthians 12-15 we will be looking at these verses more closely.

NOTE: The great debate at this point is what they were hearing. Were they hearing the tongues being spoken in the multiple dialects present or was the miracle their hearing? Whatever it was, this thing called speaking in tongues was a heavenly language being understood on an earthly level.

Bewilderment turned into amazement and marveling as they began to question what was going on.

> *"And they were amazed and marveled saying, Why are not all these who are speaking Galileans? And how is it that we each hear them in our own language (agreed upon code) to which we were born?"*

Acts 2:8

NOTE: In Genesis 11, God scattered the people because

they were speaking the same language. Many years later, those remnants of the scattered were hearing uneducated Galileans speaking their dialects. Of course, the only explanation is that they were not speaking from their intellect, they were speaking from their spirits, bypassing their minds and flowing out of their mouths. God gave them the utterance (what they were to speak) and they did the actual speaking. There will be more on this later.

In Acts 2:9-11 we see the various languages/dialects represented.

- Parthians
- Medes
- Elamites
- Mesopotamia
- Judea
- Cappadocia
- Pontus
- Asia
- Phrygia
- Pamphylia
- Egypt
- Libya
- Cyrene
- Rome (Jews and proselytes)
- Cretans
- Arabs

The question is; what were all of these people hearing in their own language?

"...we hear them in our own tongues (language/dialects) speaking of the mighty deeds of God."

Acts 2:11

MIGHTY DEEDS: Megaleios (meg-al-i'-os)= magnificent, that is, (neuter plural as noun) a conspicuous favor, or (subjectively) perfection: - great things, wonderful works. (*Strong's*)

NOTE: These 120 people filled with the Holy Spirit, speaking in a tongue/language/dialect that they did not know in the natural, were not speaking about how wonderful they were, how much better they were because they were speaking in tongues or how spiritual they were in their own self-righteousness. No, they were speaking of the wonderful, great, magnificent, perfect, conspicuous favor of God. We will examine in detail what is being spoken in a church service as we look at I Corinthians 12-13 in our next chapter.

Some of the people hearing these wonderful things of God were continuing in amazement and great perplexity saying, "What does this mean?" (Acts 2:12) Others were mocking and saying, "They are full of new (sweet) wine." (Acts 2:13)

NOTE: There is nothing new under the sun (unless you know the Son). There will always be people who may not understand what is going on, but they will be amazed as people speak about the mighty deeds of God (in tongues or in a language they understand) and there will always be the ones who mock the move of God and accuse those speaking of being drunk or deceived.

Peter took a stand upfront as spokesman of the 120 including the Eleven (with the newly elected Matthias) and spoke to the thousands with an explanation of what was taking place. The first thing that Peter set straight was that they were not drunk.

> *"But Peter taking his stand with the eleven, raised his voice and declared to them; Men of Judea, and all you who live in Jerusalem, let this be known to you, and give heed to my words, for these men are not drunk, as you suppose, for it is only the third hour of the day."*
>
> Acts 2:14-15

NOTE: The third hour of the day was 9:00 in the morning. There had to be another explanation for what was taking place other than some early morning drinking. Peter, the one who denied Jesus three times in front of men and little girls—and always flying off in a fit of rage or impetus impulses—was standing before men, not afraid, but with a power that gave Him the ability to be a witness.

THE EXPLANATION (The Joel Connection)

Peter spoke of ancient prophesy as an explanation for what was being experience in what at that time. Here is what Peter quoted from Joel 2:28-32. He was saying this is that.

> *"But this is what was spoken of through the prophet Joel; and it shall be in the last days;"*
>
> Acts 2:16

- That I will pour forth My Spirit upon all flesh (mankind)
- And your sons and your daughters shall prophesy

- And your young men shall see visions
- And your old men shall dream dreams
- Even upon My bond-slaves, both men and women I will in those days pour forth of My Spirit, and they shall prophesy
- And I will grant wonders in the sky above
- And signs on the earth beneath
- Blood and fire, and vapor of smoke
- The sun shall be turned into darkness
- And the moon into blood
- Before the great and glorious day of the Lord shall come
- And it shall be, that everyone who calls on the name of the Lord shall be saved

Peter proceeded to give a powerful message about Jesus, the condition of mankind and the solution for that lost condition. (Acts 2:22-40) Many of those present were pierced in their hearts and asked Peter and the rest of the apostles, "Brethren, what shall we do?" Peter responded,

> *"And Peter said to them, Repent, and let each of you be baptized in the name of Jesus Christ for the forgiveness of your sins; and you shall receive the gift of the Holy Spirit. For the promise is for you and your children and for all who are far off, as many as the Lord our God shall call to Himself. And with many other words he solemnly testified and kept on exhorting them, saying be saved from this perverse generation!"*

Acts 2:38-40

The cause-and-effect of this outpouring of the Promise of the Holy Spirit, and the Word of God going forth was evident in salvation and the establishment of the church.

> *"So then, those who had received his word were baptized and there were added that day about three thousand souls. And they were continually devoting themselves to the apostles' teaching and to fellowship, to the breaking of bread and to prayer. And everyone kept feeling a sense of awe; and many wonders and signs were taking place through the apostles. And all those who had believed were together and had all things in common; and they began selling their property and possessions, and were sharing them with all, as anyone might have need. And day by day continuing with were one mind in the temple, and breaking bread from house to house, they were taking their meals together with gladness and sincerity of heart, praising God, and having favor with all the people. And the Lord was adding to their number day by day those who were being saved."*

Acts 2:41-47

NOTE: This is a written snapshot of the history of the beginning of the Church. There were around one million people in town for Pentecost and of those, three thousand were saved. Many were from out of town and we see believers sharing things in common to meet the needs. This is not necessarily the stamp of approval or command to live communally but a historical perspective.

THE ACTS EXPERIENCE CONTINUES

What happened in the second chapter of Acts was not a one-time isolated incident, but was continued throughout the years. As we have implied, it does not end with the twenty eighth chapter of Acts, but continues to this day as Acts chapter twenty-nine (you and me). This includes the experience of speaking in tongues.

Let's look at the subsequent experiences of the Holy Spirit in the book of Acts. Chapters one through ten reflects a ten-year time span from the initial outpouring that did not cease then, but continued on in a few more reported events. Remember, everything that took place was not reported, just like all that Jesus did and said were not written down; but that does not mean that more events were not said or done. (John 21:24-25) Here is a recap and overview.

- John 20:22: Jesus gathered His disciples and breathed on them and commanded them to receive the Holy Spirit and gave them authority to pronounce forgiveness of sins.

- Luke 24:49: Jesus commanded them, after they had received the Holy Spirit via His breath, to go to Jerusalem and wait for the Holy Spirit to receive power to be witnesses. (Acts 1:8)

- Matthew 3:11, Mark 1:8, Luke 3:16, John 1:33: This would be Jesus baptizing them in/with/by the Holy Spirit.

- Acts 1:8: They shall receive promised power.

- Acts 2: The Promise comes like a rushing, mighty wind.

- Acts 2:16-21/Joel 2:28-32: Peter's Explanation

- Acts 4:8: Peter continues to speak filled with the Holy Spirit.

- Acts 8:12-24: The Holy Spirit received in Samaria as they were saved, baptized (in water) and they received.

- Acts 9:1-22: The persecutor of the church blinded,

healed, filled with the Spirit, saved.

NOTE: No mention of Paul speaking in tongues here, but in I Corinthians we see that he does speak in tongues. "I thank God, I speak in tongues more than you all." (I Corinthians 14:18) Again, we will be looking in depth at the letter of correction to those in the Church of God in Corinth.

- Acts 10:38, Acts 10:44-48: The Holy Spirit received in Caesarea at Cornelius' (a centurion of the Italian cohort) house.

- Acts 19:1-7: Twelve men (it does not have to be a large gathering like 120) received the Holy Spirit after they had believed.

The common thread in most of these incidences of the Holy Spirit coming was speaking in tongues. Even in those where it is not expressly seen, there is an implication that something was seen that made people desire the gift of the Holy Spirit. In the case of Paul, when a non-apostle—Ananias—laid hands on him, it was not mentioned that he spoke in tongues at the filling of the Spirit. We see later that he not only wished that everyone spoke in tongues, but that he spoke in tongues, "more than you all."

MY PERSONAL TESTIMONY

I was a member of the cradle roll, as my parents took me to church at an early age. At some point they went to church, but eventually quit going for various reasons (most likely with excuses).

As I grew up, I continued to go to a church down from

my Grandmother (on my mom's side of the family) and Aunt's house. Eventually, I stopped going. The teens that went there did not seem to have anything that I didn't have. They (my peers in school) drank, smoked, had sex and then came to church. In church they acted like saints, but lived like devil the rest or the week. There were good people at that church, good teachers, godly men and women, but I was more interested in fulfilling my desires, and God was not one of those desires.

However, I had a godly grandmother on my dad's side of the family who was praying for me.

I eventually met some guys who invited me to join a band that they were forming. Through that connection, I met Brenda and, in 1969, we began dating and got married in 1972; as of the date of this writing in 2014, we are still together.

It was through my connection with Brenda that I started going back to church. She was going all of the time and, if I was going to see her, some of that time was going to have to be in church.

As we dated, over a period of time, we began to discuss getting married. One day, while we were at Shoney's Big Boy, I was eating some onion rings, and I announced to Brenda that when we got married, that we could raise the children in any religion that she wanted to because I was a heathen and I could adjust to any religion. I sat back quiet proud of myself and took a bite of my onion ring.

Brenda answered me, "That's fine, but when the children and I die, we will be going to Heaven and when you die, you will be going to Hell."

At that point, it dawned on me that she was correct. Sitting in church, pretending that I was listening to the preacher, I actually heard the Word of God and faith came.

When I drove her home, I turned off the car, turned to her, and said, "What do I have to do to get saved?"

Being the good little Baptist girl that she was, she led me down the Romans Road to Salvation, led me in a "sinner's prayer" and then started crying as we sat there in the car in her driveway. Her mother looking out the kitchen window wondering what was going on in that 1964 Mercury Comet with the windows steaming up.

This was in the fall of 1970 and, by 1971, I was enrolled in a Bible School and move to Chattanooga. By 1972, I was a Bible School dropout and working in a factory, and getting married in July.

As I worked in this factory, I met a guy named Gary Montgomery who introduced me to a guy name Vance Akin III. Vance was an odd bird, but he was passionate about his relationship with God. He was different, not just in an odd way, but also in a godly way.

It was through Vance that I was introduced to the concept that there was something more to be experienced in my Christian walk. I was lacking something, even though I was saved, I was lacking a connection, I was lacking power. Vance introduced me to the baptism in/of/with the Holy Spirit. I hungered and for this experience. Although I knew Jesus as Lord, and I knew that, "no man can say (honestly) that Jesus is Lord except by the Holy Spirit," (I Corinthians 12:3), I wanted more.

Brenda and I were not married, but we began to attend home Bible studies, meetings at the Holiday Inn for events like The Full Gospel Business Man International (FGBMFI pronounced fig-ma-fi), Derek and Lydia Prince meetings, Kenneth Hagin, John Osteen, Don Basaham and many more.

I was very skeptical of the things that were going on but, at the same time, I really wanted to believe. I was taught from the earliest years of my church experience that things like this had ceased and that those who did these type of things were either biblically and intellectual insufficient or deceived by the d-evil or just crazy. The people that were attending these meetings were a broad range of people, from physicians, lawyers, businessmen, educators and me. They had in common a salvation experience with Jesus, a belief in the miraculous and the supernatural of God and the baptism in/of/with the Holy Spirit and speaking in tongues.

Brenda was just going along for the ride with me on my journey and—as a good little church girl all her life—she was satisfied and did not desire something more. I remember at one meeting at Holiday Inn, Derek Prince and his wife Lydia were teaching and then came time for prayer. I was still skeptical of all of this mumbo jumbo, but I wanted to see something happen close up.

At the invitation for prayer, I left Brenda in the back of the room and rushed up in order to get a better look. A few of the things I saw left a lasting impression on me until this day.

I saw people with discrepancies in the length of their legs and arms be prayed for and saw their arms and legs grow out to normal length. I began to mentally rationalize how this could be faked by adjusting your body and of course mind control. But I could not rationalize away the joy and tears of the people as they were supposedly healed.

I saw Derek's wife Lydia—who reminded me an old grandmother—moving towards someone to pray for them, with her hands outstretched, but did not touch the person. They began to fall back and it looked like they were lifted up and set down gently, with no one catching them. Again, I was up close trying to figure out where the wires were attached that gently lowered the person to the ground.

The last thing that I saw was a long haired hippy type having a demon cast out of him. It was electrifying as Derek laid his hands on the man and took authority over the demon that plagued the man. The change in the man's countenance was amazing. Again, I tried to explain it away as someone who was a plant or a shill, who was a great actor to be able to change his facial contortions into a peaceful state.

That was until the man rolled up his sleeves and showed Derek his arms and the track marks of using needles to inject drugs and said, "What about these?"

Derek said, "The Lord is going to make you whole." He laid hands on them and the track marks disappeared before my very eyes.

But I still did not receive anything that night. Later on, at another time, Brenda and I went to a Bible study to listen to a teaching tape by Bob Mumford. I really don't know what was on that tape, but I was encouraged, soaking it all in.

Again, Brenda was along for the ride because she loved

me. *Ain't love grand?* That night I took her home and returned to the site of the Bible study and sat in my car.

In my hands I held a gospel track entitled, "Seven Steps To Receiving The Holy Spirit." At 12:00 at night, I systematically went down each step.

- Step One: Confess your sin.
- Step Two: Repent of your sins.
- Step Three: Renounce any ties to witchcraft.
- Step Four: Ask for forgiveness and forgive anyone who has done you wrong.
- Step Five: Ask for the Holy Spirit.
- Step Six: Receive the Holy Spirit.
- Step Seven: Speak in tongues.

In child-like faith, I just went down the list and did everything that it said to do. When I got to step seven, I just opened my mouth and began to speak this language that flowed out of my mouth. I did not understand it, but what a release it was for me.

That happened in 1972, and I have not stopped speaking in tongues since, except for about a year of so that I totally backslid.

I do not understand how this phenomenon takes place but, even as a Speech-Language Pathologist—who has studied language development so I can evaluate and treat language disorders—I do not understand how I speak what I speak in English. One of my Speech mentors found out that I spoke in tongues and began quizzing me on how I take these thoughts and form them into words. My only answer was, "I don't know, because it is not a matter of the mind, but of the Spirit."

After that wonderful midnight experience, I picked Brenda up a couple of days later to go to yet another meeting at another Holiday Inn. To get there we had to drive down the interstate. As we were travelling along in my trusty old 1964 Mercury Comet, Brenda and I had a discussion.

ME: I received the Holy Spirit last night.
BRENDA: Oh, is that right?
ME: Yes. Do you want to hear me speak in tongues?
BRENDA: Can you do it and drive at the same time?
ME: Oh yeah. (At this point I began to fluently speak in tongues).
ME: What do you think?
BRENDA: That's nice.

At this point, Brenda still did not desire this thing that I had received. A few years later, we were part of a group of people who formed a church that was a sister church of The Lord's Chapel. It was a charismatic church. Billy Roy Moore, who was pastor of The Lord's Chapel, came that night and taught about the Holy Spirit.

Of course Brenda had the Holy Spirit at this point— because no one can say that Jesus is Lord except by the Holy Spirit. At one point, a friend's little girl had to go to the bathroom and Brenda offered to take her so she would not have to listen to the message.

A few minutes later, the mother followed them into the bathroom and asked Brenda, "Brenda, would you like to receive the Holy Spirit?"

Brenda said, "Yes." The lady laid hands on her and Brenda received the Holy Spirit with speaking in tongues.

You can't put God in a box about how, when or where people receive the Holy Spirit, because it is not about the experience, it's about the relationship between Him and you.

In our next chapter, we will look at a letter of correction from Paul to the Church of God at Corinth. We will examine I Corinthians 12-14 as one unit, verse by verse and ask the who, what, when, where, why and how questions.

CHAPTER FIFTEEN
THE LETTER OF CORRECTION
(From Disorder To Order)

"Now concerning spiritual gifts, brethren, I do not want you to be unaware (ignorant)."

I Corinthians 12:1

In Speech therapy, we use various diagnostic tools to evaluate the patient. When we determine the problem and what is the root of the problem, we don't tell the patient, "This or that is your problem with your speech, so stop talking."

No, we deal with the root of the problem, adjust and compensate for the problem and—as behaviorists—we adjust the behavior so they can speak correctly. We do not recommend cessation of speech.

Now, if the patient is doing something that exacerbates the problem, then we adjust. For example, if someone has a harsh or raspy voice or is losing his voice, we will change the vocal abuse patterns that may be causing little callouses on his vocal folds. We may suggest that he speak using easy 'vocal onset' versus 'hard glottal' attack. There may need to be temporary silent for a period of time until he learns new voice patterns.

So it is with Paul's letter of correction. Some things addressed needed to be stopped, like have sex with your father's mother (most likely step-mother). That must cease. If they were getting drunk at the Lord's Supper, then getting drunk must cease, but the Lord's Supper must not cease.

The apostle Paul is writing a letter of correction to a church in Corinth. Hmmm, can you imagine a church full of human beings that might need correction? They were a blowing and going church, but Paul was writing a letter of correction to them, dealing with multiple issues. Some of the corrections were adjustments of attitude and some were blatant sin, while others were a tweaking of order within the gathering of the saints. Some things needed to be stopped altogether, while other things were to be continued but done differently.

One thing that needed to be corrected was the issue of speaking in tongues within a service. It was not a mandate to *stop* speaking in tongues—as some would have you to believe—but a *correction* with the *expectation* to *continue* speaking in tongues. There were issues of tongues in a service, prophecy, interpretation of the tongues within a service, praying in tongues, singing in tongues and the interaction of all these things together.

Most people who are against tongues have never spoken in tongues and have been taught against tongues will usually use various verses cherry picked from I Corinthians 14 as their proof text, stating that God wants things done decently and in order, so that must mean that tongues must cease. Others use the text I Corinthians 13, stating that tongues were used to establish the Church and that the *Perfect that has come*. They point to:

(1) the formation of the Church.

(2) the completed canon (collection) of Scripture.

(3) the last apostle has died.

They state that love was perfected and that it was and is greater than faith and hope. They point out that the tongues of men and of angels become a tinkling cymbal and sounding brass so we need to quit sounding off with tongues.

To see the meaning of the tongues/gifts/ miracles/supernatural controversy, one must study I Corinthians chapters 12, 13 and 14 as a single unit.

THE CHURCH OF GOD WHICH IS AT CORINTH

Many people look down their spiritual snouts at this church because of all of the problems that they were being corrected about; but a closer look shows that they had many good points about them. I have heard some comment that part of their problem was that they were called by the wrong name. Instead of the *Church of God,* they should be called the *Church of Christ.* Well, they had plenty of problems, but their name was the least of them. Here are some good points about the Church of God in Corinth which is at Corinth found in I Corinthians 1:2-9.

- They were sanctified in Christ Jesus.

- They were saints by calling.

- They were identified with all who in every place

call upon the name of our Lord Jesus Christ, their Lord and ours.

- The grace of God was given to them in Christ Jesus.

- In everything they were enriched in Him, in all speech and all knowledge.

- The testimony concerning Christ was confirmed in them.

- They are not lacking any gift.

- They were eagerly waiting the revelation of our Lord Jesus Christ.

- They were called into fellowship with His Son, Jesus Christ our Lord.

Now I don't know about you but, from my viewpoint, that church (gathering of saints) had some good qualities.

CHAPTER SIXTEEN
GIFTS OF THE SPIRIT

"Now concerning spiritual gifts..."

I Corinthians 12:1

Paul starts off the twelfth chapter with the word "Now" to deal with the next issue of spiritual gifts. The first thing that Paul lets them know is that he does not want them to be ignorant. Oh, some versions put it a little nicer, "I do not want you to be unaware," but the word means "ignorant."

IGNORANT: agnoeo (ag-no-eh'-o)=From G1 (as a negative particle) and G3539; not to know (through lack of information or intelligence); by implication to ignore (through disinclination): - (be) ignorant (-ly), not know, not understand, unknown. (*Strong's*)

> *"Now concerning spiritual gifts, brethren, I do not want you to be ignorant through a lack of information or intelligence, so as to ignore and not know or understand spiritual gifts."*

I Corinthians 12:1
[with the expanded Strong's Concordance meaning]

The first thing Paul lets them know is that, when they were pagans, they were led astray to dumb idols but, in contrast to the fact that they were now followers of Christ, they *talk* differently.

> *"Therefore, I make known to you, that now one speaking by the Spirit of God says, Jesus is accursed (anathema); and no one can say, Jesus is Lord, except by the Holy Spirit."*
> I Corinthians 12:3

The ground work is set. In speaking of righteousness and salvation, Paul wrote in Romans 10,

> *"That if you confess (say) with your mouth Jesus is Lord, and believe in your heart that God raise Him from the dead, you shall be saved; for with the heart man believes, resulting in righteousness, and with the mouth he confesses, resulting in salvation."*
> Romans 10:9-10

> *"No one can say, Jesus is Lord, except by the Holy Spirit."*
> I Corinthians 12:3

We have seen that the people in this church are followers of Jesus and the Holy Spirit is present by their confession that Jesus is Lord.

GIFTS, MINISTRIES, EFFECTS MANIFESTATIONS OF THE SPIRIT

As we flow from the Holy Spirit-inspired confession that, "Jesus is Lord," we now come to the gifts, ministries and effects of the Holy Spirit.

NOTE: Many people in the Charismatic/Pentecostal movement claim to have a certain gift. For example, if someone prays for someone to get healed, and they actually get healed supernaturally, those praying claim to have "the gift of healing."

In reality, human beings are merely the conduits that God chooses to move through to pass on a gift to someone who needs it. The gift is merely in transit as the Spirit drops it in that person. We are what I like to call the "delivery men and women of God."

For example, healing is needed. The Spirit drops it into delivery central, where we pray for someone or we lay hands on someone and the package of healing is delivered. We no longer have the gift, it has been signed, sealed, delivered by the blood of the Lamb.

Now someone who is sensitive and obedient to the Holy Spirit may be used more than others and it looks like they have the gift, but they are merely the U.P.S., the FedEx, or the U.S.P.S. (United States Postal Service)

GIFTS: Charisma (char'-is-mah)=From G5483; a (divine) gratuity, that is, deliverance (from danger or passion); (specifically) a (spiritual) endowment, that is, (subjectively) religious qualification, or (objectively) miraculous faculty: - (free) gift. G5483: charizomai (khar-id'-zom-ahee)=Middle voice from G5485; to grant as a favor, that is, gratuitously, in kindness, pardon or rescue: - deliver, (frankly) forgive, (freely) give, grant. G5485: charis (khar'-ece)=From G5463; graciousness (as gratifying), of manner or act (abstract or concrete; literal, figurative or spiritual; especially the divine influence upon the heart, and its reflection in the life; including gratitude): - acceptable, benefit, favour, gift, grace (-ious), joy liberality, pleasure, thank (-s, -worthy). G5463: chairo (khah'ee-ro)=A primary verb; to be full of "cheer", that is, calmly happy or well off; impersonal especially as a salutation (on meeting or parting), be well: - farewell, be glad, God speed, greeting, hail, joy (-fully), rejoice. (*Strong's*)

NOTE: These are not gifts of human origin, but of the Spirit (Holy).

MANIFESTATIONS: phanero sis (fan-er'-o-sis)=From G5319; exhibition, that is, (figuratively) expression, (by extension) a bestowment: - manifestation. G5319: phaneroo (fan-er-o'-o)= From G5318; to render apparent (literally or figuratively): - appear, manifestly declare, (make) manifest (forth), shew (self). G5318:

Phaneros (fan-er-os')=From G5316; shining, that is, apparent (literally or figuratively); neuter (as adverb) publicly, externally: - abroad, + appear, known, manifest, open [+ -ly], outward ([+ -ly]). G5316=phaino

(fah'ee-no)= to lighten (shine), that is, show (transitive or intransitive, literal or figurative): - appear, seem, be seen, shine, X think. (*Strong's*)

This is what happens when the Holy Spirit moves through human beings, when God's *super* comes on our *natural*; He shines in a dark world. Here is a breakdown of the manifestation for the common good found in I Corinthians 12:4-7:

- There are varieties of gifts but the same Spirit.

- There are varieties of ministries and the same Lord.

- There are varieties of effects but the same God.

- God works all things in all persons.

- Each one is given the manifestation of the Spirit

for the common good.

I like that all of these gifts/ ministries/effects are gifts that are given for the common good, on the uncommon bad. They are not to be used as competition or spiritual arrogance.

SPIRITUAL GIFTS OF THE HOLY SPIRIT (I Corinthians 12:8-10)

Paul lists nine gifts of the Spirit that were given by the Spirit and were still active in the Church of God at Corinth. There was no inkling that they should not be working or that they should cease from working. I once heard Shelia Walsh (former co-host of the 700 Club) explain that in her home church in Scotland, these were called, "the power nine all the time." John Wimber who pioneered the Vineyard Churches, called these gifts of grace, "gracelets" as they drop from Heaven to Earth for His purposes to be manifested.

Here is the list of "the power nine all the time" that were given to individuals by the Holy Spirit; thus the term, "gifts of the Holy Spirit" also known as the "manifestations of the Spirit."

THE WORD OF WISDOM: WORD: Sophia (sof-ee'-ah)=From G4680; wisdom (higher or lower, worldly or spiritual): - wisdom. G4680: Sophos (sof-os')=Akin to σαφη□ς saphe s (clear); wise (in a most general application): - wise. (*Strong's*)

This is not wisdom attained by attending higher schools of learning. This is a supernatural gift of wisdom when you don't have insight in how to handle a situation. This is when your back is against the wall or if you are in a counseling situation or even in a work situation where you are running into a dead end that you just don't have the wisdom about how to handle a certain situation. This wisdom is through the Spirit.

THE WORD OF KNOWLEDGE: KNOWLEDGE:

gnōsis (gno'-sis)=From G1097; knowing (the act), that is, (by implication) knowledge: - knowledge, science. G1097: gino sko (ghin-oce'-ko)=A prolonged form of a primary verb; to "know" (absolutely), in a great variety of applications and with many implications (as shown at left, with others not thus clearly expressed): - allow, be aware (of), feel, (have) known (-ledge), perceive, be resolved, can speak, be sure, understand. (*Strong's*)

This gift goes hand in hand with the word of wisdom. Again, this is not a knowledge revealed by human observation but as the Holy Spirit drops in "a knowing." Many times you have a sense of knowing something about somebody or a situation and you need the wisdom about what to do about it. This knowledge is according to the same Spirit.

FAITH: pistis (pis'-tis)=From G3982; persuasion, that is, credence; moral conviction (of religious truth, or the truthfulness of God or a religious teacher), especially reliance upon Christ for salvation; abstractly constancy in such profession; by extension the system of religious (Gospel) truth itself: - assurance, belief, believe, faith, fidelity. G3982: peithō (pi'-tho)=A primary verb; to convince (by argument, true or false); by analogy to pacify or conciliate (by other fair means); reflexively or passively to assent (to evidence or authority), to rely (by inward certainty): - agree, assure, believe, have confidence, be (wax) content, make friend, obey, persuade, trust, yield.

(*Strong's*)

According to the Word, "So faith comes by hearing and hearing by the Word of God/Christ." (Romans 10:17) We know that, "the righteous shall live by faith." (Romans 1:17; Habakkuk 2:4; Galatians 3:11; Hebrews 10:38). We see that we are to "walk by faith and not by sight." (II Corinthians 5:7) And the ultimate definition of faith is that it is, "the substance of things hoped for, the evidence of things not seen or revealed to the senses." (Hebrews 11:1) If you want to please God, "without faith it is impossible to please Him…" (Hebrews 11:6)

There is a thing called "natural human faith," faith that comes by believing the Word and standing in it and then the "gift of faith." In the natural, the faith that you have is only as good as who or what you place your faith in. But, a gift of faith is something that drops in you when there is no other hope. You may be facing a horrific situation and BAM, you know that you know that you know that God is in control. Again, it is by the same Spirit.

GIFT(S) OF HEALING: iama (ee'-am-ah)=From G2390; a cure (the effect): - healing. G2390: iaomai (ee-ah'-om-ahee)=Middle voice of apparently a primary verb; to cure (literally or figuratively): - heal, make whole. (*Strong's*)

The first thing I see is that it is the "*gift* of healing;" not singular, but plural. I don't think we can limit the supernatural manifestation of healing in someone's body. I wrote a workbook called The Acts of Jesus, where we looked at the Gospels of Matthew, Mark, Luke, and John and studied the forty plus (40+) incidents of healing and deliverance and the ten (10) various methods that He used. Remember that we did not read about all that He said or did because "even the world itself would not contain the books which were written." (John 21:25) Jesus told His followers that when He left and sent back the Holy Spirit, they would do the works that He did, "and greater works than these shall he do; because I go to the Father." (John 14:12)

You just can't limit how healing will be manifested when the Holy Spirit is involved. There are definitely many human methods that have been used by God to keep this body functioning including—but not limited to—physicians and medicine, chiropractors, organic food, holistic methods including massage, acupuncture, essential oils of the Bible, etc. When I read about gifts of healing in reference to the Holy Spirit, I understand it to be a healing where all hope is gone on the human, physical level and only God could have done it.

NOTE: Any physician worth anything will admit that they do not and cannot heal, but only help until the body heals itself. They can set a bone but cannot mend the bone. A physician only practices medicine, they do not have it perfected. Where there is dis-ease, dis-order and dys-function, only God can put things back into ease, order and function. A gift of supernatural healing is where—as we have said over and over, and will most likely say it again—is where "God's super comes on your natural." (Origin unknown, but I heard Mylon LeFevre say it.)

EFFECTING OF MIRACLES: MIRACLES: dunamis (doo'-nam-is)=From G1410; force (literally or figuratively); specifically miraculous power (usually by implication a miracle itself): - ability, abundance, meaning, might (-ily, -y, -y deed), (worker of) miracle (-s), power, strength, violence, mighty (wonderful) work. G1410: dunamai (doo'-nam-ahee)=Of uncertain affinity; to be able or possible: - be able, can (do, + -not), could, may, might, be possible, be of power. (*Strong's*)

The old saying is, "If you want a miracle, you are going to have to be in a hard place where you need a miracle." Most of us want a miracle, but don't want to be in that hard place. We like our lives like we like our fast food, "fast, easy and our way." The words effecting/effect/working mean the "operation" of a miracle. The word "miracle" comes from the same word where we get the word power; "dunamis" which means "dynamic ability." We get words like dynamite from the word dunamis. God's dynamic ability really is explosive.

This is what Jesus was anointed with according to Acts 10:38, "And you know of Jesus of Nazareth, how God anointed Him with The Holy Spirit and Power/dunamis, and how He went about (effecting/working) doing good and healing all who were oppressed by the d-evil for God was with Him." [emphasis mine]

A miracle is the *possible* in the face of *impossibility*. It is where your back is against the wall and nothing more than a dynamic, abundant, powerful, strength of a mighty wonderful work will deliver you. In the fat part of the Bible—the Old Testament—people were released from bondage, but their backs were against the Red Sea as armies pressed in on them to recapture them and enslave them again. This is where a miracle was manifested with a blowing wind, parting waters and dry land to walk across, as the enemies were drowned in the closing waters. (Exodus 13-15)

Our miracles may not be that dramatic, but when there is no explanation of how you were delivered from your situation and circumstance, the blowing of the gift of the Holy Spirit can take place.

PROPHECY: PROPHECY: prophe teia (prof-ay-ti'-ah)=From G4396 ("prophecy"); prediction (scriptural or other): - prophecy, prophesying. G4396: prophe te s (prof-ay'-tace)=From a compound of G4253 and G5346; a foreteller ("prophet"); by analogy an inspired speaker; by extension a poet: - prophet. (*Strong's*)

This a gift that is dropped in by the Spirit—that the human mind cannot conceive or make up—which is a prediction about a future event. Under the inspiration of the Spirit of God, someone becomes a mouthpiece for God, usually to turn them from their ways and back to God. The prophecy may be future events occurring centuries later or impending events within the lifetime of the people.

The prophets usually get a bad rap for being negative. There can be true or false prophets. Prophets can be true and angry and get in the flesh like Jonah who prophesied the demise of Nineveh. When they repented and were not destroyed, Jonah got all upset.

Again, it is a word dropped in by the Spirit, spoken and then back to normal life. If you have to tell someone you are a prophet, you are not one. If you take great pride in the gift that the Spirit has given you to deliver, then you missed the point. If you only enjoy tearing down and not building up, you are not a prophet. If you don't include yourself in the words of correction, you are not a prophet. Later on in our study of I Corinthians 12-14 we will see

185

how tongues, prophecy and interpretation of tongues interconnect in a synergistic quality.

DISTINGUISHING/DISCERNMENT OF SPIRITS:

diakrisis (dee-ak'-ree-sis)=From G1252; judicial estimation: - discern (-ing), disputation. G1252: diakrino‾ (dee-ak-ree'-no)= to separate thoroughly, that is, (literally and reflexively) to withdraw from, or (by implication) oppose; figuratively to discriminate (by implication decide), or (reflexively) hesitate: - contend, make (to) differ (-ence), discern, doubt, judge, be partial, stagger, waver. (*Strong's*)

SPIRIT:

Pneuma (pnyoo'-mah)=From G4154; a current of air, that is, breath (blast) or a breeze; by analogy or figuratively a spirit, that is, (human) the rational soul, (by implication) vital principle, mental disposition, etc., or (superhuman) an angel, daemon, or (divine) God, Christ's spirit, the Holy spirit: - ghost, life, spirit (-ual, -ually), mind. G4154: pneo‾ (pneh'-o)=A primary word; to breathe hard, that is, breeze: - blow. (*Strong's*)

The same word for The Holy Spirit (big *S*) is the same word used for the human spirit (little *s*), and the same word used for demonic spirits (little *d* and *s*). As we walk around in this cursed and fallen world, where the d-evil is known as "the prince of the power of the air," (Ephesians 2:2) and "the god of this world," (II Corinthians 4:4) and we rub elbows everyday with un-regenerated men and women and those hu-mans who are actually under the influence or possessed by evil spirits, there is a great need for distinguishing/ discernment of spirits.

This is not human intuition or a mother's intuition, but again something dropped in by the Spirit as a gift to be able to judge the spirits that are within a certain situation. Sometimes things are so obvious you don't need a gift to know what's going on, but many times, people can cover up and act one way but be another way. Once the spirit has been discerned then the Spirit may drop in a word of wisdom on what to do about the spirit (human or demonic) that has been discerned. As we walk around this natural world, we need supernatural abilities to function.

VARIOUS/DIFFERENT/DIVERS KINDS OF TONGUES:

TONGUES: glōssa (gloce'-sah)=Of uncertain affinity; the tongue; by implication a language (specifically one naturally unacquired): - tongue. (*Strong's*)

This is what was experienced in Acts, chapter 2. They were speaking in a language/tongue that was not naturally acquired, but it was supernaturally acquired. This is where we get the word *glossolalia* which is used as a slur to those who speak in gibberish.

This is what was out of control in the Church of God in Corinth that needed to be corrected. In Paul's letter of correction, he deals with the motive of the problem, the mechanics of the problem and the use of the problem within a congregational setting and within the private setting.

The arrogance that I see in humanity is thinking that the human, fleshly, tangible reality is the only reality. If we can't see it and explain it then we can't understand it. There are various/different/diver kinds of tongues. According to some sources there are 6500 spoken languages with 2000 of those having fewer speakers than 1000 people. This does not count what people would consider dead languages. In some cultures, the clicking of the tongue in various configurations can convey thoughts.

As a Speech Pathologist who speaks in tongues in my private prayer life (and occasionally in a service), I fully endorse the concept of speaking an earthly language that is unlearned and a divine language that is unlearned. We will talk more about this but, for now, this is a gift of the Spirit dropped in as needed.

INTERPRETATION OF TONGUES:

INTERPRETATION:

herme neia (her-may-ni'-ah)=From the same as G2059; translation: - interpretation. G2059: herme neuo (her-mayn-yoo'-o)=From a presumed derivative of G2060 (as the god of language); to translate: - interpret. G2060: Herme s (her-mace')=Perhaps from G2046; Hermes, the name of the messenger of the Greek deities; also of a Christian: - Hermes, Mercury. G2046: ereo (er-eh'-o)= to utter, that is, speak or say: - call, say, speak (of), tell. (*Strong's*)

When someone speaks in a tongue and others don't understand what was spoken, it is good to have someone translate or interpret what was said so everyone can understand. I have spoken in other countries and have worked with translators. Sometimes it is translated word-for-word or, at other times, they translate the general meaning. I may have said something that took me a few minutes to say and the interpreter is able to translate in one minute.

This is in the natural, but there may be times where something is spoken and the listener hears in their own language. Later, we will be looking closer in I Corinthians 14 at the correlation between tongues and interpretation and prophecy in a service.

We have seen nine gifts that have one thing in common. They are all gifts of the Spirit. It is this one and the same Spirit that works all of these gifts, and one and the same Spirit that distributes these gifts and this one and the same Spirit that works and gives to individual human beings just as He wills.

> *"But one and the same Spirit works all these things, distributing to each one individually just as He wills."*
>
> I Corinthians 12:11

THE BODY OF CHRIST (I Corinthians 12:12-30)

This working and distributing of these nine gifts of the Spirit are to individuals who make up what is known as the Body of Christ.

The Body of Christ is one body but made up of many members of that body. The analogy is that of the human body made up of various parts which causes this one unit to function. Remember in the beginning we saw that we are a three part being moving as one unit.

> *"Now may the God of peace Himself sanctify you entirely; and may your spirit and soul and body be preserved complete, without blame at the coming of our Lord Jesus Christ."*
>
> I Thessalonians 5:23

> *"For even as the body is one and yet has many members, and all the members of the body, though they are many, are one body, so also is Christ."*

I Corinthians 12:12

The Body of Christ is comprised of many members. We usually call the gathering of saints in a local locale, the Body of Christ or the Church. Of course this thing called the Church is universal and local. People make up the body/church. How do people get into this body?

> *"For by one Spirit (Holy) we are all (collectively) baptized (dipped/immersed) into one body (of Christ) whether Jews or Greeks, whether slaves or free, and we were all made to drink of one Spirit (Holy). For the body is not one member, but many."*

I Corinthians 12:13-14

Remember when we talked about the doctrine of baptisms (plural)? John the Dipper dipped people in water as the repented in preparation for the coming King. The disciples dipped people in water as the believed and came to Jesus. The Holy Spirit dipped people into Christ (the Body of Christ). Jesus would dip people in the Holy Spirit.

In the Ephesian passage we see;

> *"...there is one body (of Christ) and one Spirit (Holy), one hope of your calling (Christ in you, the hope of glory), one Lord, one faith, one baptism (dipping into the body of Christ) one God and one Father of all who is over all and through all and in all."*

Ephesians 4:4-6 (Emphasis mine)

Many use this verse as the reason that all of the Holy Spirit you need is the one time salvation experience. For me, it really shows that the one baptism to enter into the one Body is by the Holy Spirit, but does not negate the other baptism into the Holy Spirit.

BODY LIFE (I Corinthians 12:15-27)

One you have entered into the Body of Christ by being placed there by the Holy Spirit as He immersed you into Christ (I Corinthians 12:13)—where you are in Christ and Christ is in you—then God places the members in the Body as He desires. (I Corinthians 12:18) The next bullet points will show how this body life works, not only universally but also locally. I have been to various places around the world and have been in fellowship with many people and churches as we center around and have fellowship (*koinonia*) around Christ in His body.

- The body is one but has many members.

- All the members are many they are one body.

- So is Christ (his Body) one but many.

- By one Spirit (Holy) we are all baptized into one body whether Jews or Greeks, whether slaves or free, and we were all made to drink of one Spirit (Holy).

- The body is not one member, but many.

- If the foot says, "because I am not a hand I am not a part of the body," it is not for this reason any the less a part of the body (both the foot and the hand are part of the human body).

- If the ear should say, "because I am not an eye, I am not part of the body," it is not for this reason, any the less part of the body (both the ear and eye are part of the physical body).

- If the whole body were an eye, where would the

hearing be? If the whole were hearing, where would the sense of smell be? (the eye, the ear, the nose are all part of the human body).

- God has placed the members, each one of them in the body as He has desired (the physical and body of Christ).

- If they were all one member, where would the body be?

- There are many members, but one body (physically and spiritually).

- The eye cannot say to the hand, "I have no need of you."

- On the contrary (exactly the opposite) the parts of the body that seems (appears to be) weaker are necessary.

- Those members of the body that we deem less honorable, on those are bestowed more abundant honor, and our unseemly members come to have more abundant seemliness, whereas our seemly members have no need of it, but God has so composed the body, giving more abundant honor to that member which lacked.

In the Greek culture, to whom Paul was writing to, beauty was put on a pedestal while the not-so-beautiful was on a lesser tier. We do the same thing in America.

Years ago, I heard Gary S. Paxton say that at times he, "felt like the armpit in the body of Christ, a very offensive part of the body, but a much needed part of the body."

This is funny, but some people wear their offensiveness to people as a self-appointed badge of honor, giving them the right to offend people. I believe that they may be missing the point.

- There should be no divisions in the body (physical or spiritual).

- The members should have the same care for one another.

- If one member suffers, all the members suffer with it.

- If one member is honored, all the members rejoice with it.

All of this talk about body parts, honor, weaker, stronger, divisions, caring, suffering, rejoicing is about the physical body but in analogous to the Body of Christ.

> *"Now you are Christ's body, and individually members of it."*
>
> I Corinthians 12:27

APPOINTMENTS IN THE CHURCH/BODY OF CHRIST (I Corinthians 12:28)

We have seen that the way that we got into the Body of Christ was the Holy Spirit baptized us into Him. We also see that God placed (positioned) us in the Body (of Christ) as He desired. According to I Corinthians 12:28030, God has appointed positions in the Church:

- First apostles
- Second prophets
- Third teachers

- Then miracles
- Then gifts of healings
- Then gifts of helps
- Gifts of administrations
- Various kinds of tongues

Paul then asks questions about who will do these things in the Church (the body of Christ), with the expected answer to be no.

- All are not apostles, are they? (No)
- All are not prophets, are they? (No)
- All are not teachers, are they? (No)
- All are not workers of miracles, are they? (No)
- All do not have gifts of healings, do they? (No)
- All do not speak in tongues, do they? (No)
- All do not interpret, do they? (No)

Some people use these questions and expectant answers to show that everyone does not speak in tongues. I believe these things are happening in the Church and that they have not ceased and that Paul's letter is not saying they should cease but should be done in order. I think Paul is speaking of within a Church service. This is examined more closely in the fourteenth chapter of Corinthians.

Paul encourages us to desire the greater gifts and explains that he will show a more excellent way. This leads to I Corinthians 13, a.k.a. The Love Chapter.

"But earnestly desire the greater gifts, and I who you a still more excellent way."

I Corinthians 12:31

CHAPTER SEVENTEEN
THE MORE EXCELLENT WAY
(I Corinthians 13:1-13)

"But earnestly desire the greater gifts, and I who you a still more excellent way."

I Corinthians 12:31

In I Corinthians chapter 12, Paul sets out to dissipate the ignorance concerning spiritual gifts that he saw in the church in Corinth. In I Corinthians 13, he discusses the motivation of walking in the spiritual gifts. He kicks off the chapter with a delineation of the two types of tongues: (1) of men (2) of angels.

"If I speak with the tongues of men and tongues of angels, but do not have love, I have become a noisy gong or a clanging cymbal."

I Corinthians 13:1

THE BIG "IF" (I Corinthians 13:1-3)

Chapter 13 starts with the word "If" and—over the next few verses—Paul outlines things you can do without love and the cause-and-effect of what you are without love.

- Speak with tongues of men and of angels

- Have the gift of prophecy

- Know all mysteries

- Know all knowledge

- Have all faith so as to move mountains

- Give all my possessions to feed the poor

- Deliver my body to be burned (boast)

If you have all of these things—a few of the gifts that Paul wrote about earlier—but do not have love, they are nothing and nothing but a noisy gong or a clanging cymbal.

Those who are against spiritual gifts in this day and age point out this passage as proof that God is anti-gift in the church and that they should cease and desist immediately.

LOVE DEFINED (What It Is and What It Isn't) (I Corinthians 13:4-8)

LOVE: agape   (ag-ah'-pay)=From G25; love, that is, affection or benevolence; specifically (plural) a love feast: - (feast of) charity ([-ably]), dear, love. G25: agapao   (ag-ap-ah'-o)= to love (in a social or moral sense): - (be-) love (-ed). (*Strong's*)

In the Greek language, there are many words for "love." In English, we lump all of the meanings of "love" into one word and it can be confusing. I love hot dogs, God and my wife. For more details on the words for love, see Chapter Eight: The Logos-Rhema Connection.

According to Paul, and the Holy Spirit, 'Agape' is:

- Patient
- Kind
- Not jealous
- Does not brag
- Not arrogant
- Does not act unbecomingly
- Does not seek its own
- Is not provoked
- Does not take into account a wrong suffered
- Does not rejoice in unrighteousness
- Rejoices with the truth
- Bears all things
- Believes all things
- Hopes all things
- Endures all things

The bottom line is:

"Love never fails."

I Corinthians 13:8

This thing called "love" encompasses every area of our life. The other types of love, *phileo* (brotherly love for mankind), *storge* (familial love for family), *eros* (sensual love) all must be ruled by this thing called *agape* (the God kind of love). If they are not, they are not love but lust used to consume upon our flesh. The root of our love is our love for the Father.

> *"And one of the scribes came and heard them arguing and recognizing that He had answered them well, asked Him, What commandment is the foremost of all? Jesus answered, The foremost is Hear O Israel The Lord our God is one*

Lord **(Deuteronomy 6:4 The Shema, the Jewish confession of faith),** *and you shall love the Lord your God with all your heart, and with all your soul, and with all our mind, and with all your strength. The second is this, you shall love your neighbor as yourself. There is no other commandment greater than these."*

Mark 12:28-31 [addition mine]

This thing called "love" encompasses every area of our lives but, in the context of Paul's letter, it pertains to spiritual gifts and the correction to the church of God in Corinth. Look at the various areas of correction mentioned in Paul's letter to see how love applies to each one.

- If you really love God and your neighbor as yourself, you will not be having sex with your step-mother.

- If you really love God and your neighbor as yourself, you will not be fighting about who is more spiritual and who listens to the better teacher.

- If you really love God and your neighbor as yourself, you will not be eating all the food at the love feast, leaving the people at the end of the line nothing to eat.

- If you really love God and your neighbor as yourself, you will not be getting drunk at the Lord's Supper.

NOTE: They were being chastised for taking the Lord's Supper "unworthily." This does not mean their condition was unworthy and they needed to clean up their act to participate in the Lord's Supper. The word "unworthily" is an adverb that speaks of the manner in which they take the table not the condition of their soul. If that were true, no one would be taking the Lord's Supper.

If you really love God and your neighbor as yourself, you would be doing a lot of things differently. If you really love God and your neighbor as yourself, you would not be misusing the precious gifts that He has given you, including speaking in tongues.

Concerning prophecy, tongues and knowledge in I Corinthians 13:8-10:

- If there are gifts of prophecy, they will be done away with.
- If there are tongues, the will cease.
- If there is knowledge, it will be done away.

The cessation theorist points to this passage to show that these spiritual gifts will be done away with and will cease; and they are correct. At some point, they will be done away with and will cease. Their usefulness will not be needed any longer. My contention is that *then* was not the time for them to be done away with or cease and *now* is not the time either. Why?

> *"For we know in part, and we prophesy in part;* but *when the perfect comes, the partial will be done away."*
>
> I Corinthians 13:8-10 (emphasis mine)

The bone of contention is, what is "the perfect" that is coming? Whenever it comes, we will no longer need prophecy or any of the other spiritual gifts. But, what is the perfect?

> *"When I was a child, I sued to speak as a child, think as a child, reason as a child, when I became a man I did away with childish things."*

I Corinthians 13:11

Those who claim that spiritual gifts have been done away with and have ceased point to this verse and state that those who speak in tongues are childish. But Paul is pointing out that, when the perfect comes, we will cease needing these things because we have the perfect. At that time, to continue prophesying and speaking in tongues and to continue on with any of the other spiritual gifts in the presence of the perfect would be very childish.

Apparently, the perfect had not come at the time of the writing to the church of God in Corinth.

> *"For now (at the time of the writing of the letter of correction) we see in a mirror dimly, but then face to face, now I know in part, but then I shall know fully just as I also just as I have been fully known."*

I Corinthians 13:12

Paul is contrasting the *now* and *then* of the perfect not coming at that time with the perfect that will come at some point in the future.

So, what is the perfect that is to come?

> *"But now abide faith, hope, love, these three; but the greatest of these is love."*

I Corinthians 13:13

Paul ends this whole section about the perfect coming and contrasts between *the perfect not here yet* and *the perfect that will come* with the importance of faith, hope and love, and emphasizes the greatest of the three being love.

While we are here on planet Earth, looking through the glass darkly, needing the gifts of the Spirit, waiting for the perfect to come, we need faith, hope and love. Our faith is the substance of things we hope for, the evidence of things not seen. (Hebrews 11:1) We currently walk by faith and not by sight. (II Corinthians 5:7) Our faith actually works by/through love. (Galatians 5:6) So while we are here on planet Earth, we need all three to survive.

But when the perfect comes, what we *were* looking through dimly/darkly, we will *then* see our face—and the face of the perfect—clearly. At that time we will no longer need faith for the things not seen or revealed to the senses, and we will no longer need hope or confident expectation, because what we expected will be seen.

Hope and faith will pass away along with the other spiritual gifts, but love will never pass away, because God is Love. (I John 4:8) If love passes away and does not abide forever, then so goes God. But He will abide (continue) forever and ever and ever, Amen. That is why of the three—faith, hope and love--the greater is love.

Some have said that the perfect is:

- The establishment of the Church.
- The books of the Bible brought together as one unit in the canon of Scriptures.
- The last apostle passing away.

In my humble estimation, the perfect that *is to come*, is Jesus the Christ Himself. When we are in His presence—in the presence of God, absent from the body, present with the Lord—we will be face-to-face with the *Perfect* and we will no longer need knowledge, tongues, prophesy, healing or any of the spiritual gifts that we were given to survive in this cursed and fallen world.

With that in mind, we will examine I Corinthians 14 as Paul continues with his letter of correction of handling spiritual gifts until the Perfect comes. "Come quickly Lord. Maranatha!" (I Corinthians 16:22)

MARANATHA: maran atha (mar'-an ath'-ah)=Of Chaldee origin (meaning our Lord has come); maranatha, that is, an exclamation of the approaching divine judgment: - Maran-atha. (*Strong's*)

> *"For the Lord Himself will descend from heaven with a shout, with the voice of the archangel, and with the trumpet of God, and the dead in Christ shall rise first. Then we who are alive and remain shall be caught up together with them in the clouds to meet the Lord in the air and thus we shall be with the Lord. Therefore comfort one another with these words."*
>
> I Thessalonians 4:16-18

CHAPTER EIGHTEEN
PROPER USAGE OF SPIRITUAL GIFTS
(I Corinthians 14:1-40)

We are ready to embark on the proper usage of spiritual gifts within a church service and to examine the differentiation of tongues in church and tongues in private prayers. For me, it helps when I look at the connection of I Corinthians chapters 12 and 13.

Chapter 12 ends with the statement, "But now abide faith, hope, love, these three, but the greatest is love." (I Corinthians 12:13) The key word is "now." *Now* is where they were living. *Now* is where they were being corrected. *Now* is where they were gathering as believers. *Now* is where they were misusing the gifts of the Spirit. So *now*, let's look at how to move in the gifts. Remember, the Perfect (Jesus) has not yet come *back*, then or now. We will examine this section verse by verse.

> *"Pursue love, yet desire earnestly spiritual gifts, but especially that you may prophecy."*

I Corinthians 14:1

203

In our pursuit for the greatest (love), the word "yet" (but/also/moreover) we are encouraged to pursue something else. Spiritual gifts are to be pursued and not just passively; we are to earnestly (covet, warmth of feeling) desire them. For things that some claim were/are so wrong, it appears that they were/are not wrong, but perhaps the way they were/are doing it was/is wrong. Of all the spiritual gifts, prophecy is the one Paul urged them/us to earnestly desire in order to be used within the church service.

> *"For one who speaks in a tongue does not speak to men, but to God; for no one understands, but in his spirit he speaks mysteries."*

I Corinthians 14:2 (emphasis mine)

When you speak in a tongue, the recipient of the tongues is not men; you are speaking to God. No one understands it except God. In this case, what is being spoken comes from the spirit of man (human spirit, little *s*), and what is what is understood by God is a mystery to man.

> *"But one who prophesies speaks to men for edification and exhortation and consolation."*

I Corinthians 14:3

If you want to speak to men, then prophesy. The word "but" is contrasting *speaking in tongues*—which is speaking to God—and *prophecy*, which is speaking to man. When you prophesy, you are speaking to men in a tongue/language know to the listeners for their:

1. edification/building up

2. exhortation/encouragement

3. consolation/comforting

NOTE: A gentle reminder: if you love the Lord your God with all your heart, soul, mind and strength—and love your neighbor as you love yourself—then when you prophesy, you will be edifying, exhorting and consoling others and not tearing down, discouraging and provoking.

> *"One who speaks in a tongue edifies himself; but one who prophesies edifies the church."*

> I Corinthians 14:4

Some would say that we are not to edify ourselves or puff ourselves up with pride, but we are to build ourselves up by praying in the Holy Ghost. "But you, beloved building (edifying) yourselves on your most holy faith, *praying in the Holy Ghost.*" (Jude 1:20 emphasis mine) The one who prophesies, edifies/builds up the church. You can't love someone unless you love the Lord and love your neighbor as you love yourself. This is not a selfish love but a *selfless* love. When you build yourself up by praying in the Holy Ghost, you are not puffing yourself up with pride; you are building yourself up in the Lord.

> *"Now I wish that you all spoke in tongues, but even more that you would prophecy; and greater is one who prophesies than one who speaks in tongues, unless he interprets, so that the church may receive edifying."*

> I Corinthians 14:5 (emphasis mine)

Why would Paul wish that all spoke in tongues? The obvious answer is so they would all be edified. (I Corinthians 14:4) But in a church service, the greater would be the one who prophesies? Why? So all the people in the church would be edified, exhorted and consoled. (I Corinthians 14:3)

What would put prophecy on the same level as tongues?

Ah, interpretation of the tongues. If tongues are spoken, followed by an interpretation of what was said in tongues (in a service), the end result would be edification, which would be a good thing.

1. Tongues with no interpretation = Speaking to God and edifying the individual.

2. Prophecy = Speaking to humans with edification, exhortation, and consolation.

3. Tongues + Interpretation = Prophecy and the church is edified.

"But now brethren, if I come to you speaking in tongues, what shall I profit you, unless I speak to you **either** *by way of revelation or of knowledge or of prophecy or of teaching."*
I Corinthians 14:6 (emphasis mine)

It was futile for people to just come into a church service/gathering speaking in tongues—which apparently some were doing and they were out of order. Thus, the need for Paul's letter of correction concerning spiritual gifts. He did not want his brethren to be ignorant concerning spiritual gifts. Instead of just tongues in a service, to end the futility, you could:

1. Speak by way of revelation (disclosure, manifestation, a revealing).
2. Speak by way of knowledge (a knowing).
3. Speak by way of prophecy (inspired speaking).
4. Speak by way of teaching. (instruction in doctrine).

These four methods of speaking would be in a language the people understood.

"Yet even lifeless things, either flute or harp, in producing a sound, if they do not produce a distinction in the tones, how

will it be known what is played on the flute or harp? For if a bugle produces an indistinct sound, who will prepare himself for battle?"

I Corinthians 14:7-8

Paul compares non-human musical instruments to the human interaction within a gathering of people. If people don't have some reference point to *what is being played*, then *what is being heard* will not be fruitful—that is, *pleasing*—to the hearer and help them know what to do when they hear the various meanings on the sound of a bugle.

"So also you, unless you utter by the tongue speech that is clear, how will it be known what is spoken for you will be speaking into the air?"

I Corinthians 14:9

Paul explain that this confusion happens when someone comes into a gathering and begins to speak in tongues without an interpreter. No one will know what is going on and no one will be edified except for the one speaking in the tongue. Concerning such a gathering of people, he says, you might as well be speaking into the air.

"There are, perhaps, a great many kinds of languages in the world, and no kind is without a meaning. If then I do not know the meaning of the language, I shall be to one who speaks a barbarian **(foreigner),** *and the one who speaks will be a barbarian* **(foreigner)** *to me."*

I Corinthians 14:10-11 (explanation mine)

There are 6,500 spoken languages in the world today. Each one of those languages has an agreed upon code between the people. If someone came and spoke a language that everyone did not understand, that person would be considered to be a barbarian (foreigner).

"So also you, since you are zealous of spiritual gifts, seek to abound for the edification of the church."

I Corinthians 14:12

In I Corinthians 14:1, Paul encourages us to earnestly desire spiritual gifts and in I Corinthians 14:12, he says since we are zealous of spiritual gifts, to seek to edify (build up) the church (the people in the church).

EARNESTLY DESIRE: ze loo (dzay-lo'-o)=From G2205; to have warmth of feeling for or against: - affect, covet (earnestly), (have) desire, (move with) envy, be jealous over, (be) zealous (-ly affect). G2205: ze los (dzay'-los)=From G2204; properly heat, that is, (figuratively) "zeal" (in a favorable sense, ardor; in an unfavorable one, jealousy, as of a husband [figuratively of God], or an enemy, malice): - emulation, envy (-ing), fervent mind, indignation, jealousy, zeal. G2204: zeo (dzeh'-o)=A primary verb; to be hot (boil, of liquids; or glow, of solids), that is, (figuratively) be fervid (earnest): - be fervent. (*Strong's*)

ZEALOUS: ze lo te s (dzay-lo-tace')=From G2206; a "zealot." - zealous. G2206: ze loo (dzay-lo'-o)=From G2205; to have warmth of feeling for or against: - affect, covet (earnestly), (have) desire, (move with) envy, be jealous over, (be) zealous (-ly affect). G2205: ze los (dzay'-los)=From G2204; properly heat, that is, (figuratively) "zeal" (in a favorable sense, ardor; in an unfavorable one, jealousy, as of a husband [figuratively of God], or an enemy, malice): - emulation, envy (-ing), fervent mind, indignation, jealousy, zeal. G2204: zeo (dzeh'-o)=A primary verb; to be hot (boil, of liquids; or glow, of solids), that is, (figuratively) be fervid (earnest): -

be fervent. (*Strong's*)

These words infer a passion that needs to be geared to building up of the people in the church, the gathering of people where spiritual gifts are in operation.

> *"Therefore let one who speaks in a tongue pray that he may interpret."*
>
> I Corinthians 14:13

The person who actually speaks in a tongue may be the same one who interprets that same tongue. This would be two of the nine gifts of the Spirit in operation in a church service. The word "therefore" refers back to the last statement about being zealous of spiritual gifts but seek to overflow (abound) for the edification (building up) of the church (people in the service).

> *"For if I pray in a tongue, my spirit prays, but my mind is unfruitful."*
>
> I Corinthians 14:14

So this praying in tongues is your spirit (human) praying. When we pray in a language that we know or understand, our minds are praying. When a fellow Speech-Language Pathologist found out (not that I was hiding it) that I spoke in tongues, she began quizzing me on how I did it. She wanted to know how I formed those thoughts into words. She was not mocking me but could not comprehend the process. My answer mirrored I Corinthians 14:14, "It is not a matter a mind, but a matter of the spirit/Spirit."

> *"What is the outcome then? I shall pray with the spirit and I shall pray with the mind also; I shall sing with the spirit and I shall sing with the mind also."*

I Corinthians 14:15

Paul shifts from speaking in tongues to praying in tongues and singing in tongues. I have done both in my private prayer life and in a corporate services. They are very edifying as we do what Paul said in I Corinthians 14:2; speaking (and now praying/singing) to God Himself.

When I have my back against the wall and I don't know how to pray to God, I pray in the Spirit and then I find that I can pray in English with more clarity. One book that was influential in my quest for more of God was Pat Boone's *A New Song*, which tells of his initial experience with The Holy Spirit which manifested with singing in the Spirit.

> *"Otherwise if you bless in the spirit only, how will the one who fills the place of the ungifted say the Amen at your giving of thanks, since he does not know what you are saying."*
>
> I Corinthians 14:16

I like the fact that—if they are interpreted—praying and singing in tongues are considered blessings. It is also good to know that praying and singing in tongues are considered to be giving of thanks. Again, these are taking place in the presence of someone who may not be gifted in these things.

> *"For you are giving thanks well enough, but the other man is not edified."*
>
> I Corinthians 14:17

Once again, while Paul considers singing/praying/ speaking in tongues is giving thanks, but in order to edify others you must interpret.

"I thank God, I speak in tongues more than you all, however in the church I desire to speak five words with my mind, that I may instruct others also, rather than a thousand words **(5 to 1000 ratio)** *in a tongue."*

I Corinthians 14:18-19 (emphasis mine)

In Act 9:17, Paul had hands laid on him by Ananias—who was not an apostle—and he regained his sight and was filled with the Holy Spirit. Some claim that Paul did not speak in tongues like others did throughout the book of Acts but, here in the letter of correction to the Church of God in Corinth, he reveals that not only does he speak in tongues, he speaks in tongues, "more than you all." Wow!!! The Church of God in Corinth apparently was speaking tongues a lot and Paul did it "more than you all."

When my Speech Pathology mentor asked me, "you don't speak in tongues, do you?" once again my response was taken from Brother Paul when I said, "more than you all." The 5 to 1000 ratio addresses the need to speak words that others can understand so they can be edified, exhorted and consoled in a gathering of saints.

"Brethren, do not be children in our thinking; yet in evil be babes, but in your thinking be mature."

I Corinthians 14:20

The contrast of being immature (childish) and mature (an adult) is made. Jesus made it clear that we must become like a child; "...and said, truly I say to you unless you are converted and become like children, you shall not enter into the kingdom of heaven." (Matthew 18:3) This correlates in being childlike in evil (not being mature in doing evil things) but in your thinking, "be mature" (grow up). In relation to speaking in tongues, grow up and—in a service, don't just "speak in tongues" with thousands of words—but speak maturely with five words and edify the body. Paul was encouraging and correcting them to change their way of thinking about their speaking.

> *"In the Law it is written, by men of strange tongues and by the lips of strangers I will speak to this people, and even so they will not listen to me, says the Lord."*
>
> I Corinthians 14:21; Isaiah 28:11

This is speaking a language that is strange to the receivers, and this will be God speaking to them. Even though it is God speaking, He says that they will not listen to Him. When the Spirit fell on the day of Pentecost, the strange tongues fell and, when Peter spoke, some believed and some did not believe.

> *"So then tongues are for a sign, not to those who believe,* **not** *to those who believe, but to unbelievers; but prophecy is for a sign, not to unbelievers, but to those who believe."*
>
> I Corinthians 14:22 (emphasis mine)

Tongues and prophecy are both signs. One sign is to the believers and another sign is for the unbelievers. The bottom line is that both are gifts from the Spirit and both are utilized in an assembly of people.

> *"If therefore the whole church should assemble together and all speak in tongues, and ungifted* **(those unversed in spiritual gifts)** *or unbelievers* **(those without Jesus)** *enter, will they not say that you are mad?"*
>
> I Corinthians 14:23 (emphasis mine)

This verse speaks of three groups of people:

- Believers who are versed in spiritual gifts.

- Believers who are not versed in spiritual gifts.

- Those who are not believers.

Paul is saying that if those who are believers but ungifted and those who are unbelievers hear you speaking in tongues without an interpretation, they will think you are mad, insane, crazy, cuckoo.

> *"But if all prophesy, and an unbeliever or an ungifted man enters, he is convicted by all, he is called to account by all; the secrets of his heart are disclosed; and so will fall on his face and worship God, declaring that God is certainly among you."*

I Corinthians 14:24-25

Remember that we are talking about proper operation of the gifts of the Spirit that you are to earnestly desire, in a gathering of people which include believers versed in spiritual gifts, believers not gifted in spiritual gifts and unbelievers. When the spirit of prophecy is dropped in on a person—and they begin to speak secrets that only the unbeliever would know—it will lead to an encounter with God. If only tongues were spoken with no interpretation, they would not understand, *unless* interpretation is presented which is equated with prophecy.

> *"What is the outcome then, brethren? When you assemble, each one has a psalm, has a teaching, has a revelation, has a tongue, has an interpretation. Let all things be done for edification."*

I Corinthians 14:26

The outcome would be the end result: the cause-and-effect of when people gather together. Whatever is done, it should be done for edification and building up of the people. This is the nature of body life.

> *"If any one speaks in a tongue, it should be by two or at the most three, and each in turn, and let one interpret, but if there is no interpreter, let him keep silent in the church; and let him speak to himself and to God."*
>
> I Corinthians 14:27-28

Now Paul deals with some practical application of the spiritual gifts. Some feel that they are compelled to speak in tongues or interrupt the speaker or speak at the same time. The key is it should be in order; if there is no order, then they are to keep silent in the service and speak to himself and to God.

NOTE: Many people want God to come down and speak in tongues for them. They want the Holy Spirit to grab the tongue, pull it out and wag it. But that is not the way it happens any more than the brain hopping out of the skull and pulling the tongue out to say what it is thinking. The Holy Spirit gives the utterance (or thought) and the human being—by an act of their free will—speaks.

> *"And let two or three prophets speak, and let the others pass judgment."*
>
> I Corinthians 14:29

It was not just the tongue talkers that were out of order; it appears that the prophets needed a little correction also. If you have ever been in a room where everyone is speaking at once, it does not matter if it is in tongues or in a known language; it can get confusing. After the prophets spoke, the validity of what they said was to be judged by the others.

> *"But if a revelation is made to another who is seated, let the*

first keep silent. For you can all prophecy one by one, so that all may learn and all may be exhorted;"

I Corinthians 14:30

The idea is to take turns and not to talk over one another. If you all talk at once the one seated will not learn and will not be exhorted, which is what the one who prophecies is supposed to be doing.

"And the spirits of prophets are subject to prophets."

I Corinthians 14:31

There are two views about this verse.

1. The prophets are to yield to the other prophets as they are judged about what they have said.

2. The one who is prophesying is in control of what they are doing and their human spirit must yield to the prophet, so they cannot say they could not help themselves by speaking out of order causing confusion.

"For God is not a God of confusion but of peace **(order),** *as in all the churches of the saints."*

I Corinthians 14:33 (addition mine)

People who are unversed in spiritual gifts point to this verse as the reason to stop the gifts. They say there is too much confusion with all that tongue talking. In my experience, it is usually not a mass tongue talking going on; but even if one little old lady speaks in tongues and someone interprets, some people will say there is confusion.

I Corinthians 14:34-36 speaks of a separate issue of

women in the church, which we will not deal with due to it is not about the issues of the spiritual gifts.

> "If anyone thinks he is a prophet or spiritual, let him recognize that the things which I write to you are the Lord's commandment."
>
> I Corinthians 14:37-38

Some men tend to get prideful if they consider themselves a prophet or God's mouthpiece, or they think they are something special because they speak in tongues. Their own self-importance is above the Lord. So when someone like Paul—who carries the weight of authority—speaks into their lives, they will either receive it or not be recognized.

> "Therefore, my brethren, desire earnestly to prophecy and do not forbid to speak in tongues. But let all things be done properly and in an orderly manner."
>
> I Corinthians 14:39-40 (emphasis mine)

After all of the corrections are made, the bottom line is to desire earnestly to edify, exhort and console via prophesy. The phrase that jumps out to me is "...do not forbid to speak in tongues." How can this be if tongues are so wrong? Because speaking in tongues builds up the one who is talking in tongues (talking to God) as He speaks mysteries, and the giving of thanks. So both are needed:

- Prophecy.
- Tongues and tongues plus the interpretation which is on par with prophecy.

To be decent and in order in a gathering of people does not mean to stop doing it; but to do it correctly.

This concludes a look at spiritual gifts in I Corinthians chapter twelve through chapter fourteen.

NOTE: I want to underscore that just because someone has gifts or talents, it does not make them more holy than the next person. Obviously we have seen that the church in Corinth had problems and they had the gifts in operation. Speaking in tongues is not the merit badge of maturity. Without the fruit of the Spirit the gifts are out of balance. As David Wilkerson, an Assembly of God minister, once said, "I would rather work with a turned-on Baptist than cold Pentecostal any day."

CHAPTER NINETEEN
GOD IN THE WORKPLACE

*"Whatever you do, do your work heartily, as for the Lord,
rather than for men; knowing that from the Lord you will
receive the reward of the inheritance. It is the Lord Christ
Whom you serve."*

Colossians 3:23-24

My first work experience as a child was sweeping the
floors in my grandfather's horse barn. I remember getting
all excited; I had to get up early; go to the barn; had a
broom placed in my hands and was told to start sweeping.

Well, I quickly got tired and bored and began to slack off
by playing in the loft where the hay was stored. That was
my one and only day at the horse barn. I definitely was
not working as unto the Lord; I was working as unto
myself.

Before I became a Speech-Language Pathologist, I had a
checkered history of work including but not limited to:

- Samsonite, working in Department 57 where I
  hung chairs and tables on a moving line for them
  to be painted.

- Orkin Pest Control
- Fortner Foods Commissary that supplied all food for the various Sir Pizza's in Tennessee.
- Sears Warehouse in Chattanooga
- American National Bank in Chattanooga
- Cummings Sign Company
- Back to Fortner Foods (after I backslid/fell away from the Lord)
- Tennessee Mechanical Corporation
- Boyd Janitorial Service
- Decker Construction
- Brethren Construction
- Messick Homecare Company
- Nashville Rehabilitation Hospital
- Columbia Therapy Services
- Southern Hills Medical Center
- Gentiva Home Health
- Suncrest Home Health

Each one of these jobs had good moment, bad moments and some even some ugly moments. I have met some wonderful people and some not-so-wonderful people but, along the way, my God supplied my needs according to His riches in glory.

I wish that I could say that in every job I worked as unto the Lord but alas, that was not what happened. Even now I find myself slipping and either working "for da man" or "working for myself and the money."

As a Speech-Language Pathologist I have chosen to pray for all my patients. Over the years I have seen some interesting things take place. In this chapter, I will talk share a few of the more interesting times.

HOW TO PRAY FOR AN ATHEIST

When I first meet a patient, I will get to know them, evaluate the problem and then determine the individualized treatment plan. Before I leave, or they leave, I will say to them, "I just want you to know that I pray for all of my patients and I am praying for you."

Most people respond by thanking me or saying that they sure do need prayer or that they have a lot of people praying for them. If they respond in the affirmative, I might ask if I could pray for them right then and then take their hand and pray or lay my hands on them.

In my 20 plus years as a Speech-Language Pathologist, I only had one person turn me down for prayer. Here is how it went.

Me: I pray for all my patients and I am praying for you.
Patient: I don't want your !@#$%^&*()&%$#@! prayers. I am an atheist and don't believe in your god.
Me: Well, that is O.K., we can just do speech therapy, no problem.

After a few sessions here is the conversation.

Me: I am still praying for you.
Patient: Thank you, I appreciate it.

After we discharged the patient, he returned around a year later with his handicapped brother for a videofluoroscopic swallowing study.

Patient to his brother: This is the man I told you about.
Me: Nice to meet you. I will be praying for you.

Patient and his brother: Thank you.

You never know who is hurting and what they are going through. Sometimes people will try to snap your head off.

It reminds me of a story a man named Tommy Lewis shared about a hunter and his dog. They were out hunting and the dog got his leg caught in a barbed wire fence. The hunter reached down to unwrap the barbed wire, but the dog kept trying to bite his hand. So the hunter placed the side of his gun barrel in the dog's mouth. While the dog was preoccupied biting the gun, the hunter released the dog from the barbed wire. The dog immediately ran away and hid, licking the wounds.

We don't know what pain people are in and they may try to bite you as you try to help them. If I responded to my patient by being offended and rude to him, I would have closed the door to share the Lord. I wish I could tell that the atheist got saved, but I can't; *but,* I do know that seeds were planted.

THE COMA CONNECTION

When I was working in a hospital setting, I was called up to the Critical Care Unit (CCU) to see some patients and screen other patients for potential speech therapy. I had a student with me who was doing a six week internship in order to learn about Speech Therapy in a medical setting.

The CCU area is arranged with the nurses' station in the center and the rooms around it. With such close proximity, anyone near the nurses' station would be able to see and hear what happens in each room.

The intern and I had stopped at the nurses' station and got the patients' chart. While I was reading, I noticed a neurologist go into another patient's room. This lady was in a massive coma.

A little medical lesson: there are various scales of coma levels, each one has a different description and or a different level. There is the Rancho Los Amigos Coma Scales or the Glasgow Coma Levels among others.

This patient was a Level 1-No Response: Patient does not respond to external stimuli and appears asleep. This scale, combined with review of the brain MRI showing extensive damage, was the reasoning for the phrase "massive damage" which is common terminology in the medical field.

To explain this in layman's terms, a coma scale #1 is no response and likened to being in a hole down at the bottom. The scale progresses like climbing upward out of the "coma hole" until 7 or 8 fully awake and appropriately responsive.

This lady was in a Level 1 coma. All of the tests verified that she had a stroke that affected a massive amount of her brain.

The neurologist who had walked into her room, told the husband matter-of-factly, "This is as good as she is going to get. Put her in a nursing home and get on with your life." He was essentially saying that, from what he understood from the MRI and other tests, this lady would stay in the bottom of the coma hole for the rest of her life. With that, the neurologist turned and walked out of the room, leaving the husband in an emotional hovel.

Everyone who heard this doctor's pronouncement was shocked. Even if the facts are true, there is a kinder way to tell people and not be so blunt and heartless.

There were two people near the nurses' station that day that I knew were strong believers. One was a physical therapist; he and I had prayed together for patients before. The other was a nurse who I knew prayed regularly for her patients.

The three of us looked at each other and then I turned to the student intern. She and I had already discussed prayer and the implications in the workplace. "What you are about to see," I told her, "they don't teach you in school."

The five of us went into the patient's room. I told the husband that we heard what the doctor had said and asked if he would like prayer.

His response was, "Yes, could you?" We prayed for him and then I asked him if he would like prayer for his wife.

"Yes."

I spoke to him about healing from the Bible, and went over to the bed and laid hands on her, spoke healing scriptures and then bound the spirit of death. Nothing happened immediately and, before we left, we encouraged him not to give up.

The next day I went back to CCU. The patient was awake, out of the coma and sitting up in her bed talking. Speech [therapy] was consulted for a swallowing evaluation to determine if she could eat or drink. She was then stepped down to a regular floor and soon discharge from the hospital. I saw her later in outpatient therapy for speech.

What happened? The Lord made an appearance. It was nothing that I did but everything that God did. I happened to be the available delivery man of a gift of healing distributed from The Holy Spirit. Little did the neurologist realize that The Healer had His own coma scale where the hole could not hold her down much like a tomb could not hold Jesus!

UNPLUG THE VENTILATOR

Once I received a call from a nurse to see a patient that I had evaluated; I determined that I could not be beneficial in the area of speech. The nurse wanted me to come up to see the patient as soon as possible.

I told the nurse that I had already seen the patient and that, for the time being, she was not appropriate for speech.

The nurse was adamant. "This is not a matter of speech," she said, "but a matter of salvation."

I went up to the floor. The nurse explained that she and several other nurses had been witnessing to the patient about her salvation. The lady was on a ventilator and the decision had been made to take her off of the ventilator and she would die.

The nurses did not know what to do next and wanted me to lead the lady to the Lord. I spoke with the lady, shared what they had told her and asked her if she wanted to be saved.

She nodded her head.

We gathered around, and led her in a "sinner's prayer" and she affirmed by nodding her head that she had received Jesus.

I then asked if she wanted me to pray for her healing and

again she responded yes. I quoted some healing verses, laid hands on her and we prayed for healing. Again, nothing happened, no flashes of light, no bells and whistles; just plain simple faith.

I went back the next day. The ventilator had been turned off and removed. She was sitting up in bed, alive and not dead physically, and also alive and not dead spiritually.

ON A PEG TUBE FOREVER

I saw a patient and he had been sent home with the news that he would never eat or drink by mouth again, and—for the rest of his life—he would have to be fed and given drink by a tube in his stomach, known as a Peg Tube.

Of course we prayed, did therapy and, progressively, he got better. Around a year later I was at a local restaurant when I felt a tap on my shoulder.

I turned around to see my patient's wife with a big grin on her face. She pointed over to a booth where her husband sat. The man who had been told he would never eat normally again, had the Peg Tube removed and he was eating a big hamburger and fries.

THE SPOKEN WORD

On a different occasion, I saw a patient who had a stroke with resultant aphasia (a language problem), with an apraxia (motor planning problem), along with perseveration (saying the wrong thing over and over). The patient had fallen through the medical and governmental cracks and had not had any Speech Therapy.

The patient consented to prayers being said before we began therapy. No significant progress was being made but, in each session, we would hold hands, pray and stood in faith, speaking speak for what was not as though it were (Romans 4:17).

When the therapy first began, the patient could not say sound; soon he saying sentences.

NOTE: Romans 4:17 talks about "calling things that are not, as though they were" instead of "calling things that are as if they will never change."

WHAT DOES HE HAVE FOR US NEXT

I had worked for a particular company for about a year and a half when we were informed that they would be totally closing the company. It was a bombshell and people reacted differently. Some began to cry, others cussing, others gnashing their teeth, others wanting to go out and get drunk.

Me, I called Brenda and told her that they were shutting down the company and by the end of April that I would not have a job.

Without hesitation she said, "Praise God, I wonder what He has for us next."

What He had for us next was more provision. I had been a contract worker for another company; I walked into their office, explained what was happening and they hired me.

> *"My God shall supply all your needs according to His riches in glory in Christ Jesus."*
>
> Philippians 4:19

SAY THE BOOKS OF THE BIBLE

Another patient of mine was a ninety-one-year-old lady

who had a stroke, lost memory and ability to focus and recall information.

We prayed and began a process called stimulated neuroplasticity, which is a rebounding and rewiring of the brain. We began to see her ability to remember get stronger.

This ninety one year old lady was able to recite the books of the Old Testament in order, in reverse order and then I would call a number out of order and she would plug in the correct book.

As a joke, I had told her that once she could do this, I was going to take her into a bar and makes some money off of her. She cackled.

SCHOOL DAZE

I was invited to join several other professional to speak to a class of students in graduate school. The speakers were sharing their experiences in the workplace. I was asked to share my insight into the workings of a Speech Pathologist in a medical setting.

During the talk, I discussed the various aspects of life in the hospital. Then I began to convey how I approach therapy, including prayer and the various miracles that have taken place.

When I had finished, the class gave me a standing ovation. None of the other speakers received a standing ovation.

The teacher thanked me and I went back to work at the hospital.

One of students (an older woman) came by the hospital and told me that the next class period that the teacher apologized for what I had said and commented that I was very unprofessional. She said the whole class defended me and told the teacher they like what I said about life in the real world.

That is one of the reasons that I rely on the Holy Spirit and His gifts in my work. I need words of wisdom and knowledge about what to do and how to operate. When my back is against the wall, I need a prayer language that I can pray, knowing that I am praying the perfect will of God into a matter.

TEARS IN THE HALLWAY

When I finally graduated from Middle Tennessee State University with my degree in Speech, I was on fire. I was planning to go to the University of South Carolina to get my Masters in Speech, but my dad had a heart attack and I needed to stay around Tennessee. God opened a door and I was accepted to Tennessee State University.

A little side note on this story is that when I was taking the Graduate Record Exam (G.R.E.), the exam you have to take to be accepted into a graduate program. I remember the first question/problem was a drawing of a sheet of paper with dots dividing various parts of the paper and the letters A through E dotted. The question read, "If you fold section A over section E and then fold section B over section D which section will be on top?"

I sat there and tears began to trickle down my cheek, because I had no clue what they were talking about. I could not envision what they wanted and that was only the first question. I felt so inadequate and stupid and knew I would not be getting into any graduate school.

But I persevered and, by the grace of God, I had a passing score. Now back to the story.

I had applied for financial aid so I could go to graduate school and had been approved for a certain amount of money to help me along the way. On registration day we had to go through the process of standing in long lines to receive the financial aid check.

Tennessee State University is famous for disorganization. On this particular day I stood in a line for a long, long time and, when I final reached the front of the line, I was told that I was in the wrong line and had to go to another long, long, line.

Well I did; no problem, just a glitch in the system. The problem arose when I had to go through three long, long lines and in the end still had no money.

I was *hot*!

I stormed across the campus to the Graduate School Department, where I was planning to give someone a piece of my mind.

As I entered the Graduate School Building, I needed to stop by the men's room. I walked into the bathroom, still steaming, and stood in front of the urinal fuming and fussing in my head about what I was going to tell someone. As I stood there, I looked up and, in big bold, black letters, someone had written "MY GOD SHALL SUPPLY MY NEEDS ACCORDING TO HIS RICHES IN GLORY." (Philippians 4:19)

What? That was like a slap in my face. I realized that God was in control. The bottom line is that my checks came in, the issue was resolved, and I was taught another lesson.

As I mentioned earlier, I was on fire in my educational career, and when I started graduate school, I overloaded my schedule with twelve hours instead of the recommended nine hours. I was warned, but I argued the point that I had to get on with it and I could handle it.

I was taking a class that was taught by John Ashford, the director of the V.A. Hospital Speech Department and adjunct professor at T.S.U. After the first class was over, I was over; I was overwhelmed and *over* graduate school.

After class, I was standing in the hallway after everyone had left, crying. Mr. Ashford (who is now Dr. Ashford) came out and listened graciously as I poured out my frustrated heart to him.

Long story short, I dropped out of school, defeated and discouraged.

A few years later, I still had the fire of Speech Therapy in me, and I called Mr. Ashford up and told him that I was considering returning to school and asked him what he thought.

Among other things he told me, "I think that you should do it."

I will be forever grateful to him—and to Him—for that bit of advice. I returned to school and graduated and my tears were turned to joy.

> *"...weeping may endure for the night, but joy comes in the morning."*
>
> Psalm 30:5

"...to grant those who mourn in Zion, giving them a garland instead of ashes, the oil of gladness instead of mourning, the mantle of praise instead of a spirit of heaviness, so they will be called oaks/trees of righteousness, the planting of the Lord, that He may be glorified."

Isaiah 61:3

These are just a few of the stories God has unfolded in my life. I have found that when you put God first over money, job security, position and prestige, He will always take care of you.

There is no separation of the secular and the spiritual life. There is no separation of church and state, no matter how hard people try to make it so. We started out this chapter with Colossians 3:23-24 and we will end it by breaking it down.

- *Whatever:* This is all conclusive.

- *You do:* This is your physical work.

- *Do your work:* Actively participate in it.

- *As for (unto) the Lord:* You are not working for your boss, your corporation, even to meet your needs.

- *Rather than men:* Men will disappoint, God never will.

- *Knowing that from the Lord you will receive the reward of the inheritance:* God is a rewarder and when you walk by faith, it pleases Him and He rewards those who diligently seek Him. (Hebrews 11:6)

- *It is the Lord Christ whom you serve:* Bob Dylan puts it this way, "You got to serve somebody, it may be the d-evil, it may be the Lord, but you got to serve somebody."

CHAPTER TWENTY

THE SPEECH-FAITH CONNECTION

"And Jesus replying said to them, 'Have faith in God'
(constantly)."

Mark 11:22
The Amplified Bible

Some would say that it does not take much faith to speak.
We just open our mouths and say whatever pops out.
When we swallow food, drink, medicine or saliva, we just
swallow. When we think a thought we just take it for
granted.

That is how we should flow in the Spirit as we walk by
faith and not by sight. I see a great connection between
thinking, speaking and hearing, and doing the Word of
God.

In this chapter we will be looking at this thing called faith
and how it impacts everything we do. We will be looking
at how it affects our prayers; how it affects our
confessions, declarations and affirmations; and how it
affects the way we respond to the Spirit or react in the
flesh with our speech.

When our world is shaken, our speech will manifest what

we really believed. There will come a time in our lives when we will have an opportunity to walk in a dark and lonely place between the point of prayer and the point of provision in the land called nitty-gritty. We will need to have our faith and speech connected to determine how we will walk.

The focus of this section is to emphasize the need for faith to be manifested as you are faced with the mountains of impossibilities in the areas of speech, hearing, swallowing and cognitive dysfunction. You will either muddle through the best you can with your education and certification and letters behind your name or you will rely on God. From my personal experience as a Speech-Language Pathologist, you will run into impossibilities where only your faith can see beyond the impossibilities into the possibility.

> *"For nothing will be impossible with God."*
> Luke 1:37, Matthew 19:26, Genesis 18:14
> Jeremiah 32:17, Mark 10:27, Luke 18:27

Faith is what (Who) I rely on, not only for my everyday living but also when my back is pressed against the wall by impossibilities.

IMPOSSIBLE: adunateo (ad-oo-nat-eh'-o)=From G102; to be unable, that is, (passively) impossible: - be impossible. G102: adunatos (ad-oo'-nat-os)= unable, that is, weak (literally or figuratively); passively impossible: - could not do, impossible, impotent, not possible, weak. (*Strong's*)

NOW FAITH IS

> *"Now faith is the substance of things hoped for, the conviction **(evidence)** of things not seen."*
> Hebrews 11:1 (explanation mine)

233

This is not just a blind faith, but a faith that sees beyond the physical where you are convinced, convicted and confess the Word of God.

"Now faith is the assurance (the confirmation), the title-deed) of the things [we] hope for, being the proof of things [we] do not see and the conviction of their reality—faith perceiving as real fact what is not revealed to the senses."

Hebrews 11:1
The Amplified Bible

The breakdown of this thing called faith is:

- Substance: A setting under as a support, essence, assurance, confidence.

- Assurance: Promise or pledge; guaranty; surety; full confidence; freedom from doubt; freedom from timidity; self-confidence; belief in one's abilities.

- Confirmation: Proof, conviction, to establish the truth, accuracy, validity, or genuineness of; corroborate; verify; to make firm or more firm; add strength to; settle or establish firmly.

- Title-deed: A deed or document containing or constituting evidence of ownership; a deed or document evidencing a person's legal right or title to property, especially real property.

- Things hoped for (confidently expected): to expect or confide; to anticipate, usually with pleasure; confident expectation.

- Evidence/conviction of their (the things hoped for) reality: a fixed or firm belief; the act of

- moving a person by argument or evidence to belief, agreement, consent, or a course of action.

- Faith perceives as real fact what is not seen/not revealed to the senses: to recognize, discern, envision, or understand *Senses*: any of the faculties, as sight, hearing, smell, taste, or touch, by which humans and animals perceive stimuli originating from outside or inside the body; a feeling or perception produced through the organs of touch, taste, etc., or resulting from a particular condition of some part of the body.

(*Strong's* with my thoughts)

I have to approach therapy like that all of the time. If I relied only on the facts or only on results or only on my senses, I would give up on people.

Many times after a session, I will talk with the patient and/or the family and discuss the reality of the session. They may not have made any measurable progress during the session, but I undergird the substance of things that we are hoping for and the evidence of the things not seen or revealed to our senses. At this point, I may tell them that we do not deny reality but we do deny reality's right to rule our lives. We don't go by what we see but, by faith we see the desired results.

After I finished graduate school in 1993, my first official job was at Nashville Rehabilitation Hospital. I was wet behind the ears and, even though I had finished my formal schooling, I was still in the learning process.

A lady came in with a Traumatic Brain Injury from a car accident. I was to evaluate her and then make a treatment planned based on the evaluation. This is the first time I was introduced to The Ross Information Processing Assessment, a cognitive-linguistic test which I continue to use to this day.

The patient scored severe on all ten subtests and I determined that I could not do anything with her. In my mind, my senses, my feelings and the facts, she was a lost cause.

My mentor took me aside and spoke words of wisdom, which I still follow to this day. "Rodney," he said, "never immediately put someone on the back burner." He meant, don't base your evaluation only on numbers of a test.

By faith I proceeded to treat the lady and she made progress.

Janny Grein wrote a song called "Covenant Woman." The message of the song is found in the idea that we are not to be moved by our feelings but by the Word of God, which is the only real thing.

Now, that is faith.

What is this thing called faith and its relationship with the Word of God? It is hearing or reading His Word which represents His thoughts and desires, believing the Word by trusting in, clinging to and relying on it and then acting on that Word as if it was true. It is not based on sight, sound or emotions; it is based on God Himself and the integrity of Who He is.

This chapter started out with a quote from Mark 11:22. Let's look at that again.

> *"And Jesus replying said to them, 'Have faith in God' (constantly)."*

> Mark 11:22 The Amplified Bible

We will be looking deeper at this verse in relation to how we should pray but for now, we need to see the expectancy of Jesus for His disciples and for us to "have faith." It would be a cruel thing for Jesus to have the expectancy but not give us a way to get this thing called faith.

FAITH COMES (Romans 10:5-17)

This thing called faith comes to where there was no faith. Some say that we all have a "measure of faith" but, as we will see, that is just not true. Faith has to come and it comes by a very specific means. We will also see how faith, our hearts and our speech impacts faith coming to where there is no faith.

THE MEASURE OF FAITH

Many assume that everyone on planet earth has faith. After all, doesn't Romans 12:3 verify that assumption? "...as God has allotted to each (every man) a measure of faith." (Romans 12:3, emphasis mine) We need to remember that this is being written, "...to every man among you..." (Romans 12:3) "...to all who are beloved of God in Rome, called as saints..." (Romans 1:7)

These verses were written to Christians/followers of Christ/believers—not to lost people—so all Christians have been allotted (given) this thing called the measure of faith. We will see that all men do not have faith, but faith *comes*.

NOT ALL MEN/WO-MEN HAVE FAITH

"Finally, brethren, pray for us that the word of the Lord may spread rapidly and be glorified, just as it did also with you;

and that we may be delivered from perverse and evil men; for not all have faith."

II Thessalonians 3:1-2

"Now wait just a minute," you may ask. "I thought that God had allotted to each (every man) a measure of faith."

Apparently, this measure of faith does not include perverse and evil men, for all perverse and evil men do not have faith.

FAITH COMES

Jesus told us to "...have faith [constantly]. (Mark 11:22 The Amplified Bible) We have seen that all men do not have faith, but there is a measure—an allotment—of faith for all believers. How does this faith come?

God's heartbeat is salvation for Jews and Gentiles alike. (Romans 1:16-17) This salvation can only take place by faith in the cross of Christ as He took our place and became the curse and propitiation (satisfactory substitute) for our sins. This is called the Gospel, the Good News, that we are to believe and we are to preach. As you hear the Word about the Death, Burial, and Resurrection of Jesus, this thing called "faith" comes and, as we confess and believe, comes righteousness and salvation. This is what Romans 10 is all about.

> *"For I am not ashamed of the Gospel of Christ (I Corinthians 15:1-5) for it* **(the Gospel of Christ)** *is the power* **(dunamis/dynamic ability)** *of God for salvation, to the Jew first and also to the Greek/Gentile."*

Romans 1:16 (emphasis mine)

Salvation is not limited to just an escape route from Hell. Salvation encompasses every need of mankind.

SALVATION: so te ria (so-tay-ree'-ah)=Feminine of a derivative of G4990 as (properly abstract) noun; rescue or safety (physically or morally): - deliver, health, salvation, save, saving. G4990: so te r (so-tare')=From G4982; a deliverer, that is, God or Christ: - saviour. G4982: so zo (sode'-zo)=From a primary word σω□ ς so s (contraction for the obsolete σάος saos, "safe"); to save, that is, deliver or protect (literally or figuratively): - heal, preserve, save (self), do well, be (make) whole. (*Strong's*)

To access salvation, you must have faith and faith must come. Paul's heart desire was for the Jew and Gentile's salvation (Romans 10:1) This thing called "righteousness" is to be lived by faith (Habakkuk 2:4; Romans 1:17; Galatians 3:11; Hebrews 10:38; Romans 10:5)

Righteousness that is based on faith speaks certain words. (Romans 10:6-8) Let's take a look at what this righteousness based on faith says:

- Do not say in your heart, who will ascend into heaven (that is to bring Christ down).

- Do not say, who will ascend into heaven (that is, to bring Christ down).

- It says, the word is near you, in your mouth and in your word—that is, the word of faith which we are preaching.

- That if you confess with your mouth Jesus as Lord, and believe in our heart that God raised Him from the dead, you shall be saved.

The cause-and-effect of speaking the word of faith that was preached to them is:

- For with the heart man believes, resulting in salvation.

- With the mouth he confesses, resulting in salvation.

- The Scriptures says, whoever believes in Him will not be disappointed.

- Whoever will call upon the name of the Lord shall be saved.

How does this take place? It is hinged on faith coming. How does this faith come?

> *"How then shall they call upon Him in whom they have not believed? And how shall they believe in Him whom they have not heard? And how shall they hear without a preacher?"*

> Romans 10:14

This believing is hinged on the calling, but the calling is hinged on believing (or having faith). This believing is hinged on hearing and this hearing is hinged on someone verbalizing The Word of Christ (aka the preacher).

> *"How shall they preach unless they are sent? Just as it is written, 'How beautiful are the feet of those who bring glad tidings of good things!"*

> Romans 10:15

In Ephesians, in the context of spiritual warfare, Paul requests for people to pray,

> *"...that utterance may be given to me in the opening of my mouth, to make known with boldness the mystery of the gospel, for which I am an ambassador in chains; that in proclaiming it I may speak boldly, as I ought to speak."*

> (Ephesians 6:19-20)

What is Paul speaking? That would be, "the word of faith" (Romans 10:8).

"Why," you may ask, "do people need to preach, utter, speak boldly, open their mouths and speak this thing called the word of faith?"

Well, it is hinged on righteousness and salvation; but before these two things can take place, faith must come and the route by which it comes is the spoken word.

> *"However, they did not all heed the glad tidings for Isaiah says, 'Lord who has believed our report?'"*
>
> Romans 10:16; Isaiah 53:1

Just because someone has heard the word of faith, does not mean they are saved or made righteous. They must believe (trust in, cling to, and rely on).

> *"For God so loved the world, that He gave His only begotten Son that whosoever believes in Him (Jesus and the work that He did on the cross and sealed by the resurrection from the dead) should not perish but have everlasting life."*
>
> (John 3:16)

Again, believers are allotted what is called "the measure of faith" (Romans 12:3) but not "all (men) have faith." (II Thessalonians 3:2) The word must be preached, it must be believed and received and confessed.

> *"So faith comes from hearing and hearing by the word of Christ."*
>
> Romans 10:17

The substance of things hoped for, the evidence of things not seen, comes by hearing physically with the hearing mechanism and hearing with the spiritual hearing mechanism. The spoken word about the Gospel—(1) The Death (2) The Burial (3) The Resurrection—is believed in the heart (the core of who we are) and confessed (spoken) out of hearts through our mouths with words.

Faith comes we believe/receive this and we act as if it is true, not based on our sight or things revealed to our senses, but our spirits perceiving as real fact what is not revealed to the senses. (I Corinthians 15:1-5; Hebrews 11:1 The Amplified Bible; II Corinthians 5:7; John 1:14)

As we have seen with Romans 10:13, the cause-and-effect of hearing, believing/receiving and calling on the name of the Lord is salvation.

GOD PLEASING FAITH

One would hope that this thing called faith would please the Lord. Until the point when I accepted the Lord's offer of Himself to me back in 1970, I was a man-pleaser (others and myself). I guess you could call me a Rod-pleaser. Bob Hartman, founder of the Christian rock group Petra, wrote a song called "God Pleaser," where he states that there are many people telling him how to live his life. The chorus states that he doesn't want to be a man pleaser; he wants to be a God pleaser.

That song sums it up for me.

"So, Rodney," you ask, "How can I please God?" Remember this thing called faith that we have been writing about? Well, without, it is impossible to please Him.

"But without faith it is impossible to please and be satisfactory to Him. For whoever would come near to God must (necessarily) believe that God exists and that He is the

Rewarder of those who earnestly and diligently seek Him (out)."

Hebrews 11:6

Let' break it down:

- Without faith it is impossible to please Him.
- You must come to Him believing.
- You must believe that He exists.
- You must believe that He is a rewarder.
- You must diligently seek (continually) Him and not just passively inquire.

To explain this in a different way:

- Unbelief and doubt cannot please God.
- You can't stay away from Him.
- You cannot doubt His existence.
- You cannot doubt that He is willing to reward you.

- If you seek Him and stop the first time He does not cater to your needs and manifest Himself to you, you will not please Him.

- If you just passively inquire, then *que sera sera*, you get what you sought.

THE SIGHTLESS WALK

Some call this "blind faith" and state that they will only see and believe what they can measure in a test tube. So they begin to regulate and conduct their lives on faith in themselves or science or evolutionists, or world leaders, or religions—yes, even in Christianity with its rules and regulations and denominational leanings—and they constantly find themselves being disappointed.

But this faith is not a blind faith. It is based on truth and the fact that God is not a man that He should lie. Faith is based on things hoped for (confidently expected) and evidence of things not seen. (Hebrews 11:1)

> *"For we walk by faith [that is, we regulate our lives and conduct ourselves by our conviction or belief respecting man's relationship to God and divine things, with trust and holy fervor; thus we walk] not by sight or appearance."*
>
> II Corinthians 5:7

HAVE FAITH CONSTANTLY

> *"And Jesus replying said to them, Have faith in God [constantly]."*
>
> Mark 11:22
> The Amplified Bible

We started off this chapter with this verse, and now we will look in depth at Jesus' teaching on prayer and how interconnected our faith is with how we *speak*. (After all, this book is about Speaking and Hearing the Word of God from the perspective of a Speech-Language Pathologist.) Our thoughts, words and actions are based on His thoughts, His words and His actions.

> *"I believed, therefore I speak."*
>
> II Corinthians 4:13; Psalm 116:10

THE MODUS OPERANDI

Jesus came from Heaven to planet Earth via a virgin birth. (Matthew 1:18-25; Isaiah 7:14; Luke 1:26-45) At approximately 30 years of age, Jesus was baptized and anointed with the Holy Spirit and Power (Acts 10:38;

Matthew 3:11-17) Jesus was anointed and had purpose. (I John 3:8; Luke 4:16-20) We then see this anointed purpose carried out for three years up to the point of being crucified, buried and then rising again from the dead. This was His Modus Operandi found in Matthew 4:23-24:

- Jesus was going about in all Galilee.
- Jesus was teaching in their synagogues.
- Jesus was proclaiming the gospel of the Kingdom.
- Jesus was healing every kind of disease among the people.
- Jesus was healing every kind of sickness.
- They brought to him all who were ill including, various diseases and pains, demoniacs, epileptics, paralytics.
- And He healed them.

In Matthew, Mark, Luke and John, we see this same Modus Operandi over and over again. There were recorded 40+ incidents of healing and deliverance and Jesus utilized 10 + methods to accomplish this.

APPROACHING JERUSALEM (Mark 11:1-10)

Known as the Triumphant Entry, this begins with Jesus riding into Jerusalem on the back of a colt. Many people were lining the road with their cloaks/garments and branches they had cut from the fields. And they were crying out:

> *"Hosanna! Blessed is He who comes in the name of the Lord. Blessed is the coming kingdom of our Father David; Hosanna in the highest!"*
>
> Mark 11:9-10; Psalm 118:25

HOSANNA: ho sanna (ho-san-nah')= oh save!; hosanna (that is, hoshia-na), an exclamation of adoration: - hosanna. (*Strong's*)

BLESSED: eulogeo (yoo-log-eh'-o)= to speak well of, that is, (religiously) to bless (thank or invoke a benediction upon, prosper): - bless, praise. (*Strong's*)

AND HE ENTERED JERUSALEM (Mark 11:11)

> *"And He entered Jerusalem and came into the temple; and after looking around, He departed for Bethany with the twelve, since it was already late."*

Mark 11:11

LOOKING AROUND: periblepo (per-ee-blep'-o)= to look all around: - look (round) about (on). (*Strong's*)

Jesus rode into town, goes into the Temple and looks all around. Jesus is scoping out the scene, checking out the territory. Jesus appears to be on a reconnaissance mission, to be dealt with at a later time. Once He saw what He wanted to see, He went to Bethany since it was getting late.

Reconnaissance is: *a mission to obtain information by visual observation or other detection methods, about the activities and resources of an enemy or potential enemy, or about the meteorologic, hydrographic, or geographic characteristics of a particular area.* (Reconnaissance, US Army FM 7-92; Chap. 4)

FIG TREE CURSE (Mark 11:12-14)

In Bethany, Jesus became hungry. This speaks to the human side of Jesus, who experienced the same physical things that we experience, like hunger. Sometimes we forget that Jesus *was* in the beginning and Jesus *was with*

God and Jesus *was* God. And Jesus became (human) flesh) and dwelt among us. We spiritualize Jesus as "the Teflon Savior" who was not susceptible to the things that mere mortals experience. But Jesus became hungry and thirsty, tired and weary, had to urinate and defecate, sweated and had boogers. So, "Jesus became hungry."

He spied out a fig tree in the distance that was in leaf. Jesus went to check out the tree to see if perhaps (or perhaps not) He would find anything on it. He found nothing but leaves. It was not the season for figs. Jesus then did something rather odd. He began talking to the fig tree.

> *"He answered and said to it, 'My no one ever eat fruit from you again!' And His disciples were listening."*
>
> Mark 11:14

Who was Jesus answering? He was answering the fig tree. The fig tree had spoken to Jesus by being fruitless. Jesus was responding by speaking to it. The "it" that is referred to is the physical and fruitless fig tree. As Jesus was having a conversation with the fig tree, His disciples were hearing what was being spoken as they were listening.

The question arises, "didn't Jesus know the seasons for fig trees?" Biblical scholar F.F. Bruce addresses the issue;

"The other miracle is the cursing of the barren fig tree (Mk. xi 12 ff.), a stumbling block to many. They feel that it is unlike Jesus, and so someone must have misunderstood what actually happened, or turned a spoken parable into an acted miracle, or something like that. Some, on the other hand, welcome the story because it shows that Jesus was human enough to get unreasonably annoyed on occasion. It appears, however, that a closer acquaintance with fig trees would have prevented such misunderstandings. 'The time of the fig is not yet,' says Mark, for it was just before Passover, about six weeks before the fully-formed fig appears. The fact that Mark adds these words shows that he knew what he was talking about. When the fig leaves appear about the end of March, they are accompanied by a crop of small knobs, called taqsh by the Arabs, a sort of fore-runner of the real figs. These taqsh are eaten by peasants and others when hungry. They drop off before the real fig is formed. But if the leaves appear unaccompanied by taqsh, there will be no figs that year. So it was evident to our Lord, when He turned aside to see if there were any of these taqsh on the fig-tree to assuage His hunger for the time being, that the absence of the taqsh meant that there would be no figs when the time of figs came. For all its fair foliage, it was a fruitless and a hopeless tree." (Bruce, *Are The New Testament Documents Reliable?*)

I believe Jesus was setting up the disciples for a lesson in praying. He had already scoped out the Temple and was about to go back to the Temple and get physical with a den of thieves. He would not only overturn tables, but He would be overturning their religious conventions.

THE RETURN TO JERUSALEM (Mark 11:15-19)

Jesus returned to the scene of his reconnaissance mission (Mark 11:11). As he entered the Temple Jesus:

- Began to cast out those who were buying and selling in the temple.
- Overturned the tables of the moneychangers.

- Overturned the seats of those who were selling doves.
- Would not permit anyone to carry goods through the temple.
- He began to teach and say to them,

"Is it not written, 'My house shall be called a house of prayer for all the nations? But you have made it a robbers den (a den of thieves).'"

Mark 11:17; Isaiah 56:7; Jeremiah 7:11

The cause-and-effect of Jesus' actions were:

"And the chief priests and the scribes heard this, and began seeking how to destroy Him; for they were afraid of Him, for all the multitude was astonished at His teaching."

Mark 11:18

Notice the response of the teaching of Jesus, God in the Flesh, Love incarnated, was a mixture of fear in the religious and astonishment in the common people.

RETURN TO THE FIG TREE (Mark 11:19-21)

- Evening came
- They would go out of the city
- As they saw the fig tree, they noted that it (the "it" that Jesus spoke to) was withered from the roots up.
- Seeing the fig tree triggered the memory of Jesus cursing the tree.
- Peter spoke to Jesus, "Rabbi, behold, the fig tree which You cursed has withered."
- Jesus declared:

"Have faith in God [constantly]."

> Mark 11:22
> The Amplified Bible.

JESUS TEACHES ON FAITH AND ANSWERED PRAYER (Mark 11:23-26)

I love the thread of continuity about prayer in this passage. It starts with Jesus entering Jerusalem and scoping out the Temple. He saw that it was not a house of prayer, but a den of thieves, but went out of the city only to return to give them a lesson about prayer. To get their attention, He caused a ruckus like hitting a mule in the head with a two-by-four. When He left the city, He took the opportunity to use the fig tree as tool to teach about faith and prayer.

NOTE: In keeping with the theme of this book—and how faith and prayer is a vital part of my life as a Speech-Language Pathologist—we are spending some time on faith and the correlation with prayer as it affects the physical world with our spiritual words.

THE SPOKEN WORD AND THE BELIEVING HEART (Mark 11:23-26)

Now we are getting down to the nitty-gritty of this thing called faith and prayer. When they came back from Jerusalem, they found the fig tree that Jesus spoke to withered up from the roots. What Peter found fascinating was that words spoken to what appeared to be an inanimate object had been affected. Let's see what Jesus meant when He said:

> *"Have faith in God, constantly."*
> Mark 11:22 The Amplified Bible

FAITH: Pistis (pis'-tis)=From G3982; persuasion, that is, credence; moral conviction (of religious truth, or the truthfulness of God or a religious teacher), especially reliance upon Christ for salvation; abstractly constancy in such profession; by extension the system of religious (Gospel) truth itself: - assurance, belief, believe, faith, fidelity. G3982: peitho (pi'-tho)==A primary verb; to convince (by argument, true or false); by analogy to pacify or conciliate (by other fair means); reflexively or passively to assent (to evidence or authority), to rely (by inward certainty): - agree, assure, believe, have confidence, be (wax) content, make friend, obey, persuade, trust, yield. (*Strong's*)

> "*Truly I say to you, whoever says to this mountain, 'Be taken up and cast into the sea', and does not doubt in his heart but believes that what he says is going to happen it shall be granted you.*'"

Mark 11:23

- Words are used (whoever says).
- The words are directed to an inanimate object like the fig tree (this mountain).
- The words spoken are specific (be taken up and cast into the sea).
- Doubt can occur as you speak (and does not doubt).
- Doubt or belief occurs in the heart (in his heart).
- Instead of doubting you must believe (but believes).
- Believe in what? (That what you say is going to happen.)
- Cause-and-effect of what you believe, don't doubt, and say (it shall be granted).

DOUBT: diakrino (dee-ak-ree'-no)= to separate thoroughly, that is, (literally and reflexively) to withdraw from, or (by implication) oppose; figuratively to discriminate (by implication decide), or (reflexively) hesitate: - contend, make (to) differ (-ence), discern, doubt, judge, be partial, stagger, waver. (*Strong's*)

BELIEVE: pisteuo (pist-yoo'-o)= to have faith (in, upon, or with respect to, a person or thing), that is, credit; by implication to entrust (especially one's spiritual well being to Christ): - believe (-r), commit (to trust), put in trust with. (*Strong's*)

This is an example of how to have faith in God, constantly. Jesus used the example of the mountain and sea, the things they could relate to. He continues to underscore what He said and how it relates to prayer. He opens up with the word "therefore" to relate His previous statement to what He is about to say.

> *"Therefore I say to you, all things for which you pray and ask, believe that you have received them, and they shall be granted you."*

Mark 11:24

- Therefore (because of what He just said about speaking to the mountain as an example)
- I say to you (teach)
- All things (this is the qualifier for what this applies)
- For which you pray (talking to God)
- And ask (specific things)
- Believe that you have received them (not going to receive, but have received as you prayed, asked,

and believed)

- Cause-and-effect (what you have prayed, asked and believed that you have received them, shall be granted/given/answered)

This applies to all things including fig trees, mountains, your job, relationships; all things. It appears that Jesus was relating the fig tree cursing to a religious system that had made the house of prayer into a den of thieves. The mountain looks like the impossibilities in your life, no matter how big. But the next statement speaks of a mountain that can hinder the prayers and asking.

> *"And whenever you stand praying, forgive, if you have anything against anyone; so that you're Father also who is in heaven may forgive you your transgressions, but if you do not forgive neither will your Father who is in heaven forgive your transgressions."*

(Mark 11:25)

Sometimes the mountain that we have to speak to before we attempt to move other mountains in our lives is unforgiving.

And whenever (qualifies the time this needs to be implemented.

- You stand praying (taking a stand until it is answered)

- Forgive (releasing people from what they did to you)

- Anything Against Anyone (That just about covers all bases on forgiveness)

- So (This opens the door for release to you for

your sins)

- Transgressions (sin that goes beyond known limits)

- What you refuse to do will bind you (neither will your Father forgive).

This has just been a thumbnail on this thing called faith. For me, it is very important to utilize my faith in every area of my life and not just as I sit on a padded pew within the four walls of a church building. It applies to my marriage, my child, my interpersonal relationship with others, my money, my karate and my job as a Speech-Language Pathologist. I can implement things that I learned in school but, without faith, I am really just shooting in the dark as to what will work in therapy. Of course, for faith to be effective in any arena of our lives, it must work by love. As is spoken by Paul:

> "For in Christ Jesus neither circumcision nor uncircumcision means anything, but **faith** working through **love**."
>
> Galatians 5:6 (emphasis mine)

CHAPTER TWENTY-ONE
NEXT TO FINAL THOUGHTS, FINALLY

If you are reading this chapter you have either enjoyed the book or you have merely endured the book or you have flipped to the last chapter of the book. Whatever method you chose, I am glad that you have made it.

As of this writing, I have written 62,169 words, if I believe the word counter to the left side of my screen. I remember someone saying once, when they had endured a preacher pontificating on the Bible for an hour and a half, "That's an awful lot of words when he could have just said 'Jesus.'"

In comparison, this library of books that we call the Bible, was written by 40 authors, and contains 807,361 words and all point to Jesus. I guess they could have just leather bound the one word "Jesus" but to relate to the human mind—so that we could wrap our minds around the concept of a Savior—we needed 807,361 words to paint a picture. They say (who is this 'they' that they speak of) that, "A picture is worth a thousand words." Compare that with the concept of time with the Lord and thousands of words are relatively short.

> *"But, beloved, be not ignorant of this one thing, that one day is with the Lord as a thousand years, and a thousand years as one day."*
>
> II Peter 3:8

As I put my thoughts down in this book about my vocation as a Speech-Language Pathologist, the sun is setting on my career as retirement is rising on the horizon. Oh, I have a few more years left in me, but I am anticipating one door to close and another to open.

When you have a relationship with the Creator of the universe, you are never limited with what He has in store for your life. I was talking with a patient the other day who had a miserable life and he complained, "They talk about the golden years. Well, where are they?"

He went on vocalizing his troubles and his woes (many of them self-inflicted by bad choices and poor planning over the years) and my mind flashed back to another elderly gentleman. This gentleman also had a miserable life and he was exiled into a nursing facility, with no family, declining health and a plethora of other problems. He said to me, "Rodney, grumbling and complaining is nothing but d-evil praise." What a difference a perspective makes.

> *"Rejoice in the Lord always, and again I say rejoice."*
>
> Philippians 4:4

> *"Rejoice always; pray without ceasing; in everything give thanks, for this is the will of God concerning you in Christ Jesus."*
>
> I Thessalonians 5:16-18

"And we know that God causes all things to work together for good to those who love God, to those who are called according to His purpose."

Romans 8:28

These are just a few verses that keep things in perspective for me. Here are a few life verses that also keep me grounded."

"For me to live, is Christ, and to die is gain."

Philippians 1:21

"But whatever **(my job, any talents, my education and degrees)** *were gain to me, those things* **(and they are just things)** *I have counted as loss for the sake of Christ. More than that, I count all things to be lost in view of the surpassing value of knowing Christ Jesus my Lord, for whom I have suffered the loss of all things, and count them but rubbish* **(garbage, dung, filth, dung heap, worthless, refuse)**, *in order that I may gain Christ."*

Philippians 3:7 (addition mine)

"For I am not ashamed of the **Gospel (Good News of the Death, Burial, and Resurrection of Jesus)** *for it* **(the Gospel)** *is the power of God, for salvation, to the Jew first and also to the Greek. For in it* **(the Gospel)** *the righteousness of God is revealed from faith to faith, as it is written, 'But the righteous man shall live by faith."*

Romans 1:16-17 (addition mine)

In closing of this next-to-the-final-thoughts/finally chapter, I would like to leave you with two verses that speak of words and purpose that are at the core of who I am and what I try to do with my life.

"Let no **(don't allow)** *unwholesome* **(rotten)** *word proceed from your mouth, but only such a word as is good for edification according to the need of the moment, that it may give grace to those who hear. And do not grieve the Holy Spirit of God, by whom you were sealed for the day of redemption. Let all bitterness and wrath and anger and clamor and slander be put away from you, along with all malice. And be kind to one another, tender-hearted, forgiving each other, just as God in Christ also has forgiven you."*

Ephesians 4:29-32 (addition mine)

"Whatever you do, do your work heartily **(from the soul),** *as for the Lord rather than for men; knowing that from the Lord you will receive the reward of the inheritance. It is the Lord Christ whom you serve."*

Colossians 3:23-24 (addition mine)

CHAPTER TWENTY-TWO
FINAL THOUGHTS, FINALLY

NO REALLY, FINALLY

I would be remiss if I did not tell you my story and give you an opportunity to know the basis for all (or as much as I allow) that I say or do. Back in the fall of 1970, I made a decision that would change the course of my life forever. I choose to become a follower of Jesus instead of stumbling around in the darkness of my life.

I was nineteen years old and was a fearful, paranoid, floundering human being in need of a Savior. I was playing in a band, had some great friends, a wonderful girlfriend.

The girlfriend is pivotal to my story. She was a good Christian girl who went to church all of the time. My thought process, *if I wanted to spend more time with her*, then I could score some time and some points if I went to church with her, which I did.

259

As our relationship progressed, we began talking about marriage. I have a very vivid memory of the two of us going to Shoney's Big Boy and sitting in the drive-in section, eating and talking. At one point, I told her that we could raise the children in any religion that she desired, because I was a heathen and I could adjust to any religion.

With that statement, I sat back to take a bite of my onion ring (and oh they were the best onion rings around), feeling pretty good about myself and my open-minded wonderfulness. As I crunched the onion ring, Brenda said, "Well that is fine, but when me and the children die, we will go to Heaven, but you will go to Hell and we will be separated."

Bam! At that point I didn't say much, but I know that the onion ring didn't taste as good as it did before she said that.

I drove her home and pulled into the driveway at 426 4th Avenue and parked my 1964 Mercury Comet. Normally, I would take the opportunity to get some good kissing in before saying good night, but this time I turned to her and asked, "Well, what do I have to do to get saved?"

Apparently, all my years as a child in church, and my recent going to church had an impact on me. Faith does come by hearing, and I had heard the Word.

At this point, her Sunday school training kicked in and she led me down what is known as The Roman's Road to Salvation, which is a series of verses in the Book of Romans. This was just a tool that pointed out the need and the solution and how to get saved. Here is what she told me:

> "As it is written, there is none righteous, no not one."
>
> Romans 3:10

"For all have sinned and fall short of the glory of God."

Romans 3:23

"But God demonstrates His own love toward us, in that while we were yet sinners, Christ died for us."

Romans 5:8

"Therefore, as through one man sin entered into the world, and death through sin, and so death spread to all men for all sinned."

Romans 5:12

"For the wages of sin is death, but the free gift of God is eternal life in Christ Jesus us Lord."

Romans 6:23

"That if you confess with your mouth Jesus as Lord, and believe in your heart that God has raised Him from the dead, you shall be saved; for with the heart man believes, resulting in righteousness, and with the mouth he confesses, resulting in salvation."

Romans 10:9-10

"For whoever will call upon the name of the Lord will be saved."

Romans 10:13

"For faith comes from hearing, and hearing by the Word of **(concerning)** *Christ."*

Romans 10:17 (addition mine)

Brenda then led me in what is known as "The Sinner's Prayer." Now, there is no official prayer that you have to pray.

I could have screamed out "Jeeeeesssssssuuuuuusssss" and He would known the intent of my heart, but I had to believe in my heart that God raised Him from the dead and I had to confess with my mouth Jesus as Lord. This prayer helped to guide me in that.

If you desire a relationship with God, and you believe the Gospel, the Good News about the Death, Burial and Resurrection of Jesus and you want to confess with your mouth, this is as good as any time or place to do it. (Read I Corinthians 15:1-3 for the 'Gospel in a Nutshell'). Pray this prayer:

Jesus, I come to you confessing my sins, realizing that I am in need of a Savior. I really do believe in my heart that You took my place on the cross and paid a debt that I could never pay. I really do believe that You died on that cross; that You were buried as a dead man; and that You rose again on the third day. I really do believe that as I accept what You did and believe and confess it, that I too will be raised again to walk in newness of life. I pray this in Jesus' name. And now Lord, as I have prayed this in faith, I will act as if it is a true fact.

> *"Therefore, if any man/**wo-man**/**hu-man** is in Christ, they are new creations, the old things passed away, behold, new things have come."*
>
> II Corinthians 5:17 4 (emphasis mine)

AND IN CONCLUSION
YES, I LIED ABOUT THAT FINAL WORD THING

You have just finished reading a book--a story—really, a travelogue about my journey as a follower of Jesus the Christ, also known as a Christian, and how my faith intertwined with my vocation.

Some would like to separate their *religion* from their *work*. They like their *real life* that they live six days a week separate from their *religious life* they live on one day out of the week. Some call it the *secular* versus the *religious*. But I am of the mind-set that you cannot separate the two.

In my book, I correlate Speech-Language Pathology with my Christianity; but, I truly believe that you too could write a book how you live your faith out loud in your work setting. Here are a few verses that I use as a guideline to live my life.

> *"And whatever you do in word* **(what you say)** *or deed* **(what you do),** *do all* **(everything)** *in the name of the Lord Jesus, giving thanks through Him to God the Father."*
> Colossians 3:17 (emphasis mine)

*"Whatever you do, do your work heartily **(from the soul);** as for the Lord, rather than for men; knowing that from the Lord you will receive the reward of the inheritance. I it is the Lord Christ whom you serve. For he who does wrong will receive the consequence of the wrong which he has done, and without partiality."*

Colossians 3:23-25 (emphasis mine)

"Whether, then, you eat or drink or whatever you do, do all to the glory of God."

I Corinthians 10:31

"Whoever speaks, let him speak, as it were, the utterances of God, whoever serves, let him do as by the strength which God supplies, so that in all things God may be glorified through Jesus Christ, to whom belongs the glory and dominion forever, and ever. Amen."

I Peter 4:11

*"Slaves **(employees),** be obedient to those who are your masters **(employers)** be obedient to those who are your masters (employers) according to the flesh, with fear and trembling, in the sincerity of your heart, as to Christ; not by way of eye service, as men-pleasers, but as slaves of Christ, doing the will of God from the heart. With good will render service, as to the Lord, and not to men, knowing that whatever good thing each one does, this he will receive back from the Lord, whether slave or free."*

Ephesians 6:5-8 (emphasis mine)

Here is the bottom line that will spill over into everything that we do; our love for the Lord, our love for ourselves, and our love for others, as we live our faith out loud and love passionately. In response to a question about which was the greatest commandment, Jesus underscored how powerful love is to accomplish the purposes of God.

> *"Jesus answered, he foremost is Hear, O Israel; the Lord our God is one Lord, and you shall love the Lord your God with all your heart, and with all your soul, and without all your mind, and with all our strength. The second is this, you shall love your neighbor as yourself. There is no other commandment greater than these."*
>
> Mark 12:29-31; Deuteronomy 6:4-5; Leviticus 19:18

ABOUT THE AUTHOR

Rodney Boyd is first and foremost a follower of Jesus Christ. He is also a husband, dad and speech-language pathologist. Rodney holds a Master's Degree in Education with emphasis in Speech Communication and has been a practicing Speech-Language Pathologist since 1993. He holds a 2nd degree Black Belt in Wado Ryu Karate; has a passion for music of all styles; and enjoys writing, teaching the Word of God.

Rodney has been married to his high school sweetheart, Brenda, for more than 40 years and together they have one son, Phillip.

Boyd bases his life on Colossians 3:17, "And whatever you do in word or deed, do all in the name of the Lord Jesus, giving thanks through Him to God the Father."

Also Available From

WordCrafts Press

Pro-Verb Ponderings
31 Ruminations on Positive Action
by Rodney Boyd

Never Run A Dead Kata
by Rodney Boyd Ni Dan

Morning Mist
Stories from the Water's Edge
by Barbie Loflin

Why I Failed in the Music Business
and how NOT to follow in my footsteps
by Steve Grossman

Youth Ministry is Easy!
and 9 other lies
by Aaron Shaver

Chronicles of a Believer
by Don McCain

Illuminations
by Paula K. Parker & Tracy Sugg

www.wordcrafts.net

53194726R00155

Made in the USA
Middletown, DE
26 November 2017